THE BEST DEFENSE
A COMPLETE GUIDE TO PERSONAL AND HOME DEFENSE

Michael D. Janich

Other books by Michael D. Janich:
Advanced Fighting Folders (video)
Blowguns
Breath of Death (video)
Bullseyes Don't Shoot Back
Contemporary Knife Targeting
Fighting Folders (video)
Forever Armed (video)
Homemade Martial Arts Training Equipment
Junkyard Aikido (video)
Knife Fighting
Making It Stick (video)
Martial Blade Concepts, Volumes 1-5 (videos)
Mastering Fighting Folders (video)
Mastering the Balisong (video)
Mook Jong Construction Manual
Practical Unarmed Combatives, Volumes 1-3 (videos)
Silat Concepts
Street Steel
Warrior Path

The Best Defense: A Complete Guide to Personal and Home Defense
By Michael D. Janich

Copyright ©2013 Michael D. Janich
All rights reserved.

ISBN 978-1-939467-00-3
Printed in the United States of America

Published by Martial Blade Concepts LLC
1716A North Main Street
PMB 206
Longmont, CO 80501 USA

All rights reserved. Except for use in a review, no portion of this book may be reproduced in any form without the express written permission of the publisher.

Neither the author nor the publisher assumes any responsibility for the use or misuse of the information contained in this book.

Visit our web site at www.martialbladeconcepts.com.

DISCLAIMER

The information contained in this book is provided for academic purposes only. It is not intended to replace hands-on instruction with a qualified instructor. Do not attempt any of the techniques or skills demonstrated in this book without the supervision of a professional instructor.

It is the reader's responsibility to research and comply with all applicable laws regarding the use of force in self-defense and the possession, ownership, and carry of weapons. The author, publisher, and distributor of this book disclaim any liability for the use or misuse of any information presented in this book.

CONTENTS

Dedication	7
Acknowledgments	9
Foreword	11
Foreword	13
Introduction	15
Chapter 1: Home Security	17
Chapter 2: Home Defense and Safe Rooms	29
Chapter 3: Home Invasions	37
Chapter 4: Awareness, Avoidance, De-escalation, and Boundary Setting	41
Chapter 5: Empty-Hand Tactics	47
Chapter 6: Improvised Weapons	55
Chapter 7: Flashlight Tactics	61
Chapter 8: Defensive Use of the Cane	69
Chapter 9: Pepper Spray Basics	75
Chapter 10: Knives and Self-Defense	81
Chapter 11: Point Shooting—The Heart of All Shooting Technique	89
Chapter 12: Carjacking Defenses	95
Chapter 13: Workplace Violence	101
Chapter 14: Self-Defense for the Physically Challenged	107
Chapter 15: Safety in the Back Country	113
Conclusion	115
Resources for Further Study	117

DEDICATION

This book is dedicated to all those who have accepted that they are responsible for ensuring their own safety and the safety of their families and have taken action to prepare themselves for that challenge. Your astute grasp of reality and your dedication to the spirit and skills of self-reliance set you apart and will serve you well.

ACKNOWLEDGMENTS

I would like to express my sincere thanks to everyone involved in the production of *The Best Defense* TV show for your outstanding support and teamwork, including Michael Bane, Rob Pincus, Mike Seeklander, Tim Cremin, Matt Shults, Brandon Greene, Kevin Gellis, Rob Stookey, Derek Orr, Darlene Marshall, and Denise Jackson. To my co-hosts Rob Pincus and Mike Seeklander, thank you for sharing your knowledge and skills with me and our viewers. It is an honor to be associated with you and *The Best Defense* project.

To my students and training partners, thank you for your continued support and brotherhood—as well as your services as "meat puppets" and "bruise monkeys" during the development of my curriculum.

Most importantly, to my wife Sally and my daughter Lauren, thank you for believing in me.

FOREWORD

When I look back over the highlights of my career in the firearms training industry, there is no doubt that my work with Mike Janich and Michael Bane on *The Best Defense* ranks right up there near the top.

When Michael Bane reached out to me in 2008 to see if I was interested in doing the show with him, one of the big selling points was the opportunity to work with Janich. I knew that we would be able to work together to create compelling and informative content and bring enough difference to the material, while still agreeing on fundamental principles, that there could be an interesting interaction for the viewer.

What I did not know was how much fun it would be. While Janich and I been friends and worked on a couple of projects over the years, we hadn't really ever spent significant amounts of time together and neither of us had worked on a show quite like *The Best Defense* before. In fact, it became clear quite early on that *The Best Defense* wasn't going to be like any other previous firearms show that had been produced. A key element in the shows appeal became the hypothetical scenarios that Janich, Bane and I would script out and then role-play as part of our discussion of "bad, better and *best*" choices during dynamic critical incidents. Acting out the roles of both the bad guys and the good guys was something that Janich and I really were able to have some fun with. In fact, I think Janich really enjoyed kicking the crutch out from under me during Season 3. I think he also enjoyed hitting me in the back of the head when we fought at my favorite bar in Virginia. I *know* he enjoyed rolling my seemingly lifeless body down into the roadside ditch when we taped in Colorado in 2010.

I had my fair share of fun too... usually pretending to shoot him for one thing or another. The scenes that stand out the most, however, were the fake arguments that we'd need to have from time to time to create the precursors to an attack by a bad guy. Going from "Where are we eating tonight?" to a heated argument about absolutely nothing that led to knives, guns and impact weapons or any other array of fake physical violence was always a good time.

Of course, as much fun as it was, the focus was always on the content. The reason that *The Best Defense* is a highlight of my career is not because I got to work with friends or that we had good time doing it, it is because of the incredible number of people who have told me how much they got out of those shows. Even after millions of DVDs being sold, over a decade of live training and hundreds of articles and training video clips being produced, *The Best Defense* stands out as some of the most often mentioned material that I know impacted people, made them safer, and motivated them to think more deeply about their defense and that of their families.

I am thrilled that Mike has taken the time, effort and energy to produce this book. Having authored a couple myself, I know that the process isn't nearly as much fun as fake arguing with your friend in front of cameras. It's a lot of work to present information about chaotic, surprising and dynamic situations and how you can best prepare to survive them in book form, especially when you have to live up to the quality established by the TV production. Luckily, Mike is a master communicator and a gifted instructor. It was an honor to have worked with him on the show and to have been any part of the value that you will gain from reading this book.

Rob Pincus
I.C.E. Training Company

FOREWORD

I remember meeting Mike Janich at the SHOT Show in Las Vegas sometime around the 2007 timeframe at the Blackhawk booth. I had watched Mike in numerous training videos and wanted to shake his hand. I remember thinking that the cliché rang true: the quieter, less assuming individuals are often the ones most skilled in their trade. In Mike's case he is one of the best martial artists in the country, and more specifically a guy who knows his blades much better than most.

What I didn't realize at that time was that years later I would be given the opportunity to work with Mike extensively as one of the co-hosts on the TV show *The Best Defense*. You may think that given that opportunity, I would learn a bunch of knife techniques from Mike. While that is certainly the case, what absolutely amazed me was the fact that when I got to know Mike Janich, I found him to be literally an encyclopedia of knowledge about EVERYTHING related to self-defense. I had no idea the depth of knowledge that he possessed about pretty much every subject out there.

I am well known as a firearms instructor, have spent years shooting and training with firearms, and would like to think I have a solid body of knowledge about that subject. But as Mike and I filmed for the various shows for *The Best Defense*, I found was learning more about shooting and the integration of the firearm than I had in years....from the "knife guy!" Working and training with Mike was truly an eye opener, and I am sure to continue to learn from him in the future. By reading this book, so will you!

As Mike and I got to know one and another, we developed a friendship as well as a desire to ensure that we relayed the best possible techniques to the viewers of the show. In doing so we often got into lengthy discussions about technique, what works, and what doesn't. I found these discussions to be eye opening because Mike did what he does best: <u>he made me think</u>. Often times real self-defense is about "thinking," and the person who out-thinks the other will most likely survive the situation. Mike is incredibly skilled with a gun, knife, improvised weapons, and even his hands and feet, and as an excellent instructor he can relay those skills to you. More importantly, the biggest thing you will get from Mike is a body of knowledge relayed in a clear manner that will make you think. He is the most knowledgeable individual I have ever met when it comes to the dynamics of personal self-defense.

Take this book, read it, absorb the information and utilize the techniques. Most importantly, think about what you read and apply the information Mike is relaying to keep yourself and your family safer. I can tell you, without a bit of reservation, that what you are reading is *the* definitive guide to defending yourself. There is no better material, or author to write it, so take Mike's advice and use it to create your own best defense!

Mike Seeklander
Shooting-Performance

INTRODUCTION

When Michael Bane asked me if I wanted to be involved in *The Best Defense* television show back in 2008, I was both honored and extremely excited. The opportunity to be a part of a television production was, in itself, pretty amazing. However, for me, the greater opportunity was the ability to share my approach to personal and family protection with a broad audience through a very powerful medium.

Since becoming involved in the show, the feedback I have received from viewers has been incredible. The most gratifying comments I've received have been from couples and families who watch the show together and, for the first time, take an active family-oriented approach to self-protection. Along with their appreciation, they have consistently expressed an interest in learning more about the topics we address on *The Best Defense* and digging deeper than the show's format will allow.

The greatest challenge we face during the production of the show is packing as much information and readily understandable instruction into the 19 minutes we have available per episode. That limitation and my desire to overcome it was the inspiration for this book. It was originally intended as a co-authored work with my first co-host, Rob Pincus. Unfortunately, due to his other teaching and business commitments, he withdrew from the project. Nevertheless, his insights into personal defense and tactical training and the collaborative spirit with which we approached the first three seasons of the show are strongly reflected herein.

Readers should note that the original format for *The Best Defense* series emphasized Rob's instruction in firearms tactics and my instruction in the strategic aspects of self-defense, unarmed tactics, and the use of contact-distance weapons. Although we did follow that approach in general terms, we also tried to introduce as much "cross-over" as possible to highlight the fact that the best defensive skill set is an integrated skill set. When Mike Seeklander joined the series in the 2011 season, we made an even more concerted effort to blur the lines between empty-hand skills and firearms. Nevertheless, out of respect for Rob and Mike's roles as lead firearms instructors in the series—as well as their respective approaches to shooting skills and firearms tactics—I have chosen not to focus heavily on shooting instruction in this book. Rather than teaching how to shoot, I chose to address the contextual dynamics of different self-defense scenarios and what you need to consider to use firearms safely and effectively in those situations.

I have also added some supplemental information on my approach to shooting that was not included in the series—again in deference to Rob's and Mike's contributions to the show. Specifically, I have added my perspectives on point shooting—based on my work with the late close-combat legend Col. Rex Applegate and the late Jim Cirillo—and my personal approach to integrating point shooting, sighted fire, and contact-distance combative handgun skills.

For further information on the shooting skills highlighted in *The Best Defense*, I strongly suggest that you supplement your training with books, videos, and personal instruction with both Rob Pincus and Mike Seeklander. They are both truly world-class instructors and I recommend them and their materials very highly.

I sincerely hope that this book helps you further your self-defense training and that it becomes a useful resource for developing sound personal-protection habits for you and your loved ones. Thank you for your interest, support, and confidence.

Stay safe,

Michael Janich
March 2013

CHAPTER 1: HOME SECURITY

No matter where you live, your home should be a safe haven for you and your family. Once inside, you should feel safe and secure, protected from the threats of the outside world. Unfortunately, violent home invasions are becoming increasingly frequent and are happening in even the best neighborhoods. And because of this threat, we all need to take a hard look at our home security and develop sound family-defense plans.

The Best Defense against a home invasion is making your home a hard target. This is accomplished in two basic ways: enhancing the physical security of your home and establishing and following sound family security rules.

Hardening Your Home

Your first priority in keeping your family safe should always be to invest in the external security of your home. Good physical barriers and warning systems will ideally deny criminals entry to your home completely. If they try, they simply fail to get in. Unfortunately, achieving absolute protection against criminal entry is difficult, and, unless your home is purpose-built with that kind of security in mind, often impossible. However, that doesn't mean that it isn't worth the effort make your physical security as good as it can be.

Even if your home isn't completely invulnerable, sound physical security will provide a significant challenge that will slow criminals down, call attention to their actions, and give you and your family time to react appropriately—all worthy goals. The time, effort, and noise it requires for an intruder to penetrate the *outer* layers of your home's defenses gives you the opportunity to collect your family and retreat to a reinforced *inner* area. It also gives you the time to call 911 and access weapons to defend yourself.

Good external physical security is also important because it has a great deterrent effect. In addition to making entry more difficult, the investments you make in physical security will also send a strong message to anyone even considering your home as a target, hopefully convincing them that they are better off looking for easier targets.

There are a number of key elements to a good home security system. Although the exact needs of your home or apartment may vary, you should consider all the following aspects of home "hardening" and address them as appropriate.

First of all, you should take a look at your home from a criminal's point of view and assess it from the outside. This assessment should include close scrutiny of your exterior lighting. By illuminating the exterior of your home, especially with motion-activated lights mounted high enough so they cannot be tampered with, you can prevent criminals from approaching your home unnoticed and deny them hiding places around your home. If the cost of having an electrician install hard-wired security lights is prohibitive, consider solar-powered security lights. They operate the same way as wired lights, but charge via an attached solar panel.

Your front door is an important part of your home security. Glass windows are an easily exploited weak point.

These can be placed virtually anywhere there is adequate sun exposure during the day and are very reasonably priced.

Many home invasions begin with the criminal simply kicking in your front door. Amazingly, most of the locksets and mounting hardware you'll find on typical homes provide very little protection against this type of entry. A good, hard kick will easily break the door stile or the frame where the lock's strike plate is anchored. This can happen so quickly and so suddenly that you have very little time to react and nobody outside your home really notices what's happening. The best way to prevent this type of entry—and a great way of establishing your home as a hard target—is to harden your front door.

First, choose a sturdy, solid-wood door or a steel-sheathed door. Although decorative doors with windows in them are attractive, they are also extremely vulnerable. To gain entry, a criminal only has to break the glass in the door and reach through to open it from the inside. Again, this can happen very quickly and is likely to go unnoticed by your neighbors, so don't compromise. Get a sturdy, solid front door.

Just as important as the door itself is the hardware used to mount it. Your door should be hung with heavy-duty hinges installed with extra-long screws (like three-inch deck screws), not the short ones that typically come in the package. To further strengthen the hinge side of the door, at least one screw in each hinge should be replaced with a security hinge screw or a similar arrangement to create a "pinned" hinge. A security hinge screw looks like a traditional wood screw, except that the head of the screw is extended above the countersunk portion to form an integral pin. When installed in the hinge, the pin extends about $3/8$-$1/2$-inch above the surface of jamb side of the hinge and "nests" into the matching hole in the door side of the hinge. This reinforces the hinge joint in the closed position and prevents the door from being removed—even if the hinge pins are removed.

If you can't find purpose-designed security screws, you can easily make your own by replacing one hinge screw with a steel nail, a piece of all-thread, or a long lag screw. To do this, remove one of the screws from the jamb side of each hinge and the matching screw from the door side. If using a nail, cut the head off the nail and file the end smooth. Install the nail into the hole in the jamb side of the hinge, leaving about ½-inch extending above the surface of the hinge plate. When you close the door, the exposed portion of the nail should "nest" in the hole in the other side of the hinge. If necessary, ream that hole with a drill to accept the pin.

My preferred method of pinning a hinge is to use a long lag screw, like a 4-5-inch long ¼-inch lag screw. The advantage of this type of screw is that it screws through the door jamb into the actual framework studs around the door, significantly reinforcing the strength of the door. Lube the screw lag threads with soap and use a ratchet wrench to install it through the hinge hole, leaving just over ½-inch of the shank above the surface of the hinge. Cut off the hex head of the screw (a Dremel tool helps a lot here) and grind the end of the screw shaft smooth. Trim as necessary and/or ream the corresponding hole on the door side of the hinge until the door closes smoothly.

With the hinge side of the door reinforced, it's time to turn our attention to the lock side. Don't settle for an ordinary door knob lock for your front door. These are weak and can be easily defeated. The security of your front door should only be trusted to a high-quality, name-brand deadbolt lock with a one-inch bolt throw. The interior side of the lock should be a knob style; it should not be double keyed. Removal or loss of the internal key could prevent you from being able to leave your home in an emergency, so stick with a knob. If you do not have a steel-sheathed door, the area of the door around the lock should also be reinforced with a metal door reinforcement. This adds significantly to the strength of the door structure, reinforcing the stile at its weakest point where it is drilled to accept the lock hardware.

In order for a dead bolt lock to do its job, it must anchor solidly to the door frame. The typical strike plate included with most locks is not up to this task. Instead, you need to invest in an extended, high-security strike plate. These strike plates are typically about 8-10 inches long, include multiple holes for mounting the plate, and include extra-long screws that anchor the plate solidly into the framing structure *behind* the door frame, not just the wood of the jamb itself. Remember, many home invasions begin with the criminal simply kicking in the front door, so a high-security strike plate is a must.

You should also ensure that there are no weak spots around the door that would compromise its function. The most common example of this is a window located immediately adjacent to the door. Although this window does offer the

A steel-sheathed front door or a sturdy solid-core door provides the foundation for good physical security.

 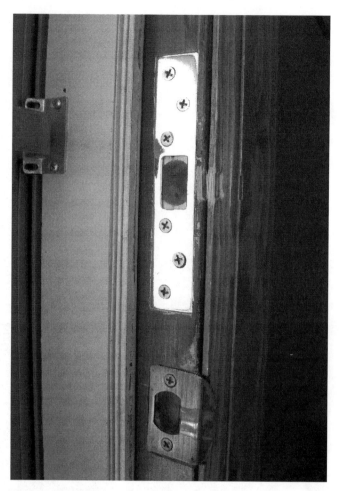

Your door is only as strong as the hardware that secures it. A high-quality dead-bolt lock is a must. By itself, the knob-style lock (bottom) is inadequate.

Just as important as the lock is the strike plate into which it anchors. Invest in a large, reinforced strike plate and anchor it to the structural studwork around the door with extra-long screws.

positive function of allowing a view of anyone standing outside your door, it compromises your security significantly. By simply breaking the window, a burglar or home invader can easily reach through and unlock the door.

The presence of a window adjacent to your door frame also means that you do not have a solid structure around the entire frame. This weakens the overall structure of the door and its function as a barrier. The "give" that exists in a poorly structured door frame leaves it vulnerable to a "jimmying" attack with a pry bar. Inserted between the door and the jamb, the bar is levered to literally spread the two apart until the bolt clears the strike plate.

Ideally, a weak door frame structure should be eliminated by having a competent contractor "fill in" that area with a solid structure. Brick, sturdy wood framing or even glass or plastic blocks can significantly increase your front-door security. If this is not possible, you should at least prevent someone from being able to access the lock if he breaks the window by covering the interior of the window frame with a sheet of strong Plexiglas® or Lexan® plastic, screwed firmly into the wood.

Once you have strengthened your front door and its mounting hardware, make sure that you have a clear view of anyone who might be standing outside that door. If you do not have a

The hinge side of the door should also be reinforced. Replace standard screws with long screws that anchor into the studs surrounding the doorway. Use a long screw or nail to create a "pinned" hinge so the door cannot be lifted from its hinges.

Windows around the frame of a door weaken the door's structure and can be easily broken, allowing the lock to be opened from the inside.

clear view from a window, make sure you install a peephole in the door or a convex mirror that allows you to see that blind spot from a window.

Obviously, if you have any other ground-level or easily accessible exterior doors in your home, you need to take the same steps to strengthen them that you did for your front door. Criminals will seek the path of least resistance, so don't leave any weak spots in your defense.

While we're on the topic of exterior doors, we should address screen doors, storm doors, and true security gates. Homes in many areas of the country have external screen or storm doors that provide an additional layer of insulation and offer the option of allowing fresh air into the house when the front door is left open. Although these doors may include locks and latches that are supposed to deter unauthorized entry, they do not offer any real security and can easily be defeated.

True security gates are made of steel, are equipped with deadbolt locks, and are installed with solid hardware that is anchored to the structure around the doorway. Done right, they are truly capable barriers and a great addition to your home security. And although they can serve as screen doors on steroids, allowing you to leave your front door open and still maintain security, why risk it? Lock both doors and find a safer way to catch a breeze.

Sliding patio doors are a weak link in a home's defenses and should receive attention to bolster their security. The traditional broomstick-in-the-track method of blocking these doors is a good start, but many criminals are wise to this and have figured out how to "rock" the sliding door to overcome this barrier or lift it out of place by snaking a piece of wire under the door. A better solution is a purpose-designed security bar that can be wedged between the door and the frame above floor level. This creates a much stronger barrier and cannot be dislodged or overcome as easily as a dowel rod or broomstick.

Aftermarket bolt-style locks can also be mounted on sliding doors to increase their resistance to forced entry. These locks are mounted on the frame of the door at the top and/or bottom. The bolts extend into holes drilled in the frame surrounding the door, providing a very secure lock-up that keeps the door from being opened or lifted out of its tracks.

One other potential weak point of home security is an attached garage. If a criminal can get into your garage, he can hide from view and can take his time getting through the door into the house. To eliminate this vulnerability, start by reinforcing the door that leads from the house to the garage, treating it exactly the same as you would your front door. If your garage has a walk-through door, apply the same security standards to it as well. Next, take a hard look at the windows and make sure they are not vulnerable to entry. If necessary, they can be barred with security bars, steel grates, or even pieces of steel angle iron.

One of the most common methods of gaining entry into garages targets those with automatic garage-door openers. In this method, the criminal pushes the top center of the door in and wedges it with a doorstop to create a small space between it and the top of the doorframe. He then fishes a long wire hook through the hole and uses it to snag the cord for the manual release. This cord, which typically has a red plastic handle on it, is attached to a latch that joins the door linkage to the drive chain. If the

Sliding patio doors are a definite weak point in a home's security. Although a broomstick in the door track can be effective, criminals have learned how to defeat it. A better choice is a purpose-designed security bar like this one from Master. It adjusts easily to fit different door sizes.

power goes out, pulling this cord releases the door linkage from the drive and allows the door to be opened manually. Pulling it with a wire from the outside works just as well and with practice can be accomplished in about 10 seconds.

To prevent this type of entry, run a zip tie through the toggle of the latch and secure it to the shuttle piece immediately above it. This makes it impossible to release the latch even if you pull on the cord. If there's a power failure, snip the zip tie, open the door, and replace the zip tie when you're done. You can also just

Another way to secure a sliding patio door is with a bolt-style lock that anchors into the door frame. These are very inexpensive and easy to install.

Automatic garage door openers typically have a manual release that allows the door to be opened during a power outage. Criminals have learned how to release these from the outside with a wire coat hanger. To prevent this, secure the linkage of the manual release with a zip tie.

remove the cord and handle from the latch and store them separately. If you need them, attach them and use them only when necessary.

For extra security when you're in your home, you can also install manual bolt-style latches that lock your overhead garage door to the roller track, making it impossible to raise the door. These are also a great idea when you're on vacation or away from home for extended periods.

Ground-level windows or easily accessible second-story windows (like those with a balcony or adjacent roof area) should also be evaluated as potential weak points. Although strengthening glass is always going to be a challenge, it can be done. The best way is the addition of 3M Scotchshield®–a reinforcing film that transforms ordinary glass into a form of safety glass. The underlying glass will still shatter, but the window remains as a barrier in the window frame. An alternative is to replace the ordinary glass with shatter-resistant Plexiglas® or Lexan®.

Windows that slide open either vertically or horizontally should have secure locks that prevent entry from outside. To supplement these, you can also pin your windows or block them from opening with wooden dowels. Pinning a window is done by drilling a small hole through the window frame into the matching framework behind it and inserting a nail or steel pin through both holes. Alternately, you can drill a hole above the frame of the closed window and insert a pin to block it from opening. The exact approach you take will depend on the construction of your windows. If you opt for the pinning method, make sure you drill carefully, staying away from the edges of the glass pane and ensuring that you don't drill completely through the frame to the outside.

An easier method to secure your windows is by wedging wooden dowels between the closed window and the opposing edge of the frame. I use ¾-inch or 1-inch hardwood dowels and carefully cut them to length to achieve a snug fit. To ensure that I can remove them quickly if necessary (for example, to use the window as an exit during a fire), I drill a hole through one end and install a short loop of parachute cord or wire. This creates a ring that provides a solid purchase to pull the dowel free. It also means that, if an intruder does make it into the house, I have pre-positioned readily available impact weapons in every window.

You can also harden your windows by adding a true barrier, like steel bars or an ornamental grate. Again, you must make sure that you do not compromise your own safety in case of a fire. Make sure that any window you might need as a fire exit remains functional.

Another excellent way of strengthening your home's external security is to invest in an alarm system. Although the alarm itself will not defeat a criminal's attempts to get into your home, it will serve to warn you, your neighbors, the alarm company, and the police of any attempts to enter. A good, professional alarm system installer will do a critical analysis of your home and recommend the types of sensors most appropriate for your situation. When they install your system, they will also walk you through its capabilities and proper operation. Take advantage of that opportunity and ask questions that are relevant to your needs and personal habits. That's the best way to ensure that you can make the most of the system and your investment.

Although the expense of installing an alarm system is significant, most insurance companies will give you a discount on your home policy if you have one. Many alarm systems also include smoke alarms and medical alert alarms, so they offer benefits far beyond crime prevention alone.

If you live in an apartment or condo or rent a home, you may not be allowed to install a

The locks on sliding windows do not offer much security. To secure these windows, cut a piece of wooden dowel and wedge it between the window and the frame. To ensure that you can remove the dowel if necessary, add a loop of cord to one end. In addition to securing your windows, these also provide you with a handy improvised weapon in every window.

centralized alarm system. However, that doesn't mean you have to do without one. A number of security companies manufacture inexpensive "stick-on" alarms that can be selectively installed on windows and doors. Each alarm unit consists of an alarm module and a matching magnet attachment. Both have double-sided adhesive tabs that allow you to stick them to doors and windows. Place the alarm unit on the door immediately adjacent to the frame and install the magnet module right next to it on the frame. With the door closed, turn the alarm on. When it is opened, the separation of the alarm unit and the magnet sets off the alarm.

These alarms are usually sold in packs of four and are primarily a means of warning you of an intrusion. While they may alert neighbors or scare off a determined home invader, their primary function is to alert you to the problem so you can react appropriately.

If you really cannot afford to invest in an alarm system (or even if you can), consider getting a dog. Dogs make great "natural" alarm systems and can be a powerful deterrent to potential burglars and home invaders. Make sure you "announce" the presence of your dog with an appropriate "Beware of Dog" sign on your fence, and a water dish and a few dog toys in your yard. A large, imposing dog with strong protective instincts obviously adds an additional layer of deterrence to your home-defense system, but don't underestimate the value of a smaller dog's abilities as an early-warning system. Learn to read and trust their reactions and investigate anything they consider suspicious.

When it comes to hardening your home, remember that perception is reality. If investing in an alarm system and/or a dog simply will not work for you, do the next-best thing and create the impression that you have made that investment. Get the sign, a few dog toys, and a water bowl and leave them where they're visible. Buy signs and window decals from an alarm company and put them up to make people believe that you do have an alarm. Create the perception that your home *is* a hard target and use it as a deterrent. Don't, however, use this strategy as your only defense. You should still invest as much as possible in *real* physical security measures.

A high-quality alarm system is an excellent investment that significantly enhances your home's security. Professional installers can configure it to suit your family's lifestyle and your home's configuration.

If you live in an apartment or condo, or you simply can't afford a professionally installed alarm system, invest in do-it-yourself alarm systems. These battery-powered alarms have adhesive mounts and can be easily installed on doors and windows. They emit a loud noise that will let you know something's wrong and may deter a home invader, but they do not signal the police.

Alarm systems are also a powerful deterrent to criminals looking for easy targets. Make sure they know you have one.

One very important home defense tactic that can be every bit as effective as an alarm system is getting to know your neighbors. By simply making the effort to introduce yourself to your neighbors, you can potentially form a strong home-defense alliance. Let them know that you would appreciate them keeping an eye on your home and that you, as a good neighbor, will do the same for them. Exchange contact information and encourage them to let you know if they see anything unusual around your house. Also, let them know that if anything ever happens to them, they should come to you for help and a safe haven. They will almost certainly extend the same offer to you.

If you have a Neighborhood Watch in your area, join it and participate actively so you know what's happening around you. If you don't, start your own or at least create a functional substitute in your immediate area. There is power in numbers.

Making and Following Rules

Home invasions typically happen in one of two ways: The invader either breaks in by defeating the physical security of your home or you "allow" him to enter by having inadequate security or falling victim to a ruse. Increasing the physical security of your home is a big step toward keeping yourself and your family safe, but no physical barrier will work if it's not used properly. The second step to keeping your family safe at home is therefore to establish a clear set of security rules and to make sure that you follow them religiously.

One of the simplest, yet most often violated rules is to simply lock your doors and windows. Many home invasions and burglaries can be prevented by just using the existing physical security measures properly. Although at first this may seem inconvenient, with a little practice and diligence, good security habits become second nature. And compared to the guilt of "allowing" someone to invade your home by leaving your guard down, such habits are worth their weight in gold.

Establish a mental checklist of the procedures you should take to maximize the use of your physical security. Every time you enter and leave your home, take a moment to pause and go through that checklist. This repetition will help you and your family members develop good security habits and make them part of your everyday routine. Work together with your family to stay consistent and do not allow yourselves to skip steps or get lazy.

Many home invasions begin with a ruse of some sort. The home invader poses as a salesperson, repairman, stranded motorist, or some other plausible role to earn your trust and get you to lower your guard and open your door. When you do, he seizes the opportunity and

Home Security

forces his way in.

Opening your door for *anybody* can leave you vulnerable to a home invasion, so don't do it. Remember, you have NO obligation to open your door for anyone. If you can't just ignore them, tell them *through the locked door* to leave information for whatever they are peddling at your door or in your mailbox. If they need help, offer to call a tow truck or whatever else they might need for them, but do not open the door to allow them to use your phone.

In case you're wondering about door chains and the sliding bars that allow you to open the door "just a bit" to talk to someone, don't waste your money—or your confidence—on them. Once you unlock your dead bolt, you're vulnerable. At that point an angry 12-year-old can kick the door hard enough to break the security chain, so don't trust them and don't get in the habit of using them.

If you choose to invest in an alarm system, learn to operate it properly and use it consistently. Many people only activate their systems when they leave their homes or go to bed. If you are home and have no immediate plans to leave, there's absolutely nothing wrong with turning on the alarm to give yourself a very significant extra layer of security. In the event of a determined home invasion, the alarm will give you an early warning to prompt your reaction plan, it will alert the alarm company to call the police, and it may scare off the intruders.

In addition to various types of sensors, most alarm systems also have manual activation options to summon the police, fire, or emergency medical services. Study the manual and talk to your installer so you know how to operate these options. Also, incorporate manual alarm activation into the steps of your home defense reaction plans and practice those plans regularly.

One final, yet very important, rule of home defense is to never discuss your home security plans with anyone outside your family. This includes sharing keys, security codes, or *any* knowledge concerning your plans or tactics with any person outside your family. You never know who could repeat such information or potentially use it against you, so keep it to yourself.

Establish good security rules and stick to them.

CHAPTER 2: HOME DEFENSE AND SAFE ROOMS

If someone does manage to gain entry to your home, the primary thing that you need to remember is that *nothing in your home is worth dying for*. Your only objective is to keep yourself and your family safe. With that goal in mind, you need to have plans of action that you can implement immediately. If you haven't thought these plans through in advance, you are not prepared. Period.

The two basic tactical choices that you will have in the event of a home invasion are to either escape out another exit and seek safety away from your home or to retreat to a "safe room"—a reinforced stronghold inside your house. It is also possible to stand and fight at the point of entry or elsewhere in your house, but even that fight should be regarded as a means to create an opportunity for the other two tactics. Remember, your safety and the safety of your family members is the ultimate goal. And the best ways to achieve that are to either leave the house or hunker down in a room that you create specifically to provide that safety.

In considering your choices of tactics, you need to take a hard look at the layout of your home, the available exits and entrances, the number of people in your family, and the way that your family is dispersed among the rooms of the house. Taking all that into consideration, you need to think about two basic plans of action: the "Fire Drill" and the "Reverse Fire Drill."

The Fire Drill is exactly what it sounds like—a plan of action that allows all members of your family to quickly and efficiently exit your home and reassemble somewhere safe. Since the dynamics of doing this are pretty much the same whether the threat is a fire or a violent invader, the drill truly does serve double duty. It also allows you to address the idea of responding to a home invasion with your family without scaring them or making them paranoid. Once they're comfortable with the general idea of getting everyone out of the house quickly and safely in the event of any emergency, you can focus on the differences between the two. That way they will understand the difference between taking the time to feel a door for heat or crawling to avoid smoke and fleeing at top speed to get away from a potentially violent threat.

Since every home and every family will be slightly different, there is no way to create a single formula for a fire drill. However, in general terms you want to think about creating a clear system of plans and simple verbal commands to implement those plans. For example, let's consider a response to a fire or home invasion threat located near the front door of your house. If the most logical thing to do is to get everyone to flee out the patio door that leads to the back yard, you should craft a plan to do that. The commands to implement that plan would be either "Fire!" (obviously, for a fire threat) or "Out!" (for any other threat). That command should be immediately followed by "Back yard!" or just "Yard!" Other exits would have simple, clearly identified names like "garage" or "front."

With this approach, everyone knows what to do (get out) and where to do it (which exit). The key to making it all work is ensuring that everyone learns to react and follow instructions immediately, not to ask what is going on.

In a home invasion situation, remember that there may be more than one attacker involved. As such, make sure the first person leaving the house through the designated exit takes a moment to look out the door or window for other threats before opening it. Incorporate back-up routes into your plan and practice them as well.

Your Fire Drill plan should also include a specific rendezvous point for the family to meet and a protocol to ensure that everyone is accounted for. Ideally, you should have already developed a good relationship with your neighbors so you can rally at one of their houses to seek immediate safety, shelter, and an opportunity to call 911.

Although fleeing your own house in response to a home invasion may seem counterintuitive or even defeatist, you need to remember that your safety and the safety of your family are always paramount. Again, *nothing in your home is worth dying for*.

The reciprocal to the "Fire Drill" is the "Reverse Fire Drill." Basically this is a carefully planned retreat to a stronghold within your home like a safe room. By getting everyone into the safe room and locking the door, you use the physical barrier it provides to keep yourselves safe while you call 911, manually activate your alarm (if you have one), and wait for help. If the barrier offered by your safe room is not adequate to hold off the home invader(s) indefinitely, it should at least buy you the time and opportunity to arm yourself—preferably with a firearm—take up a position of cover, call 911, and be prepared to defend yourself if necessary.

As with a fire drill, the reverse fire drill should be initiated with a simple, clear, verbal command like "Safe!" or "Safe Room!" and there should be a plan to account for all family members in the home before securing the door.

The "Reverse Fire Drill" is a practiced plan to retreat to your safe room. Practice it regularly and start from different areas of the house.

Home Defense and Safe Rooms

The Safe Room

Many people base their safe room planning on the stereotypical "bump in the middle of the night" scenario. They assume that the criminal will break in while they're asleep, so they choose the master bedroom as the safe room. Their plan is to get the kids into the safe room, lock the door, and call the cavalry.

While that's not a bad plan, it doesn't consider other common home-invasion scenarios and does not address initiating the plan from different locations in the house. A better approach is to look at the overall layout of your home and likely entry points for bad guys. First, determine the greatest weaknesses in the exterior physical security of your home and consider them as the entry points. Then, look at the areas where you and your family spend the most time and start considering the options for safe room locations. For example, let's assume your master bedroom is located at the far end of the house and you and your family spend most of your time in the family room. Between the family room and the master bedroom are glass patio doors that are the most likely entry point for a criminal. During a home invasion, you don't want to run past the likely entry point to the far end of the house to get to safety. A smarter plan would be to create a safe room closer to the family room and away from the patio doors.

If you have a large home or your family tends to spend lots of time at opposite ends of the house, there may not be a single, perfect location for a safe room. Instead, you may need to build two safe rooms and adjust your reaction plan accordingly.

Before you head for the home improvement store, you really need to think your family's habits and the layout of your home to determine the best location for a safe room or rooms. As part of that process, you should also consider the physical abilities and limitations of your family members. Making grandma run up two flights of stairs to the safe room doesn't make sense. Plan smarter and, if necessary, adjust the organization of your home to support your plan.

Building Your Safe Room

Once you've determined which room will serve as the basis of your safe room, you need to look at its physical structure—especially the structure of the doorway. When I decided to invest in safe room construction in my home, I enlisted the help of my friend Don Vaughan, an expert in home renovation with 25 years of experience in the installation of custom doors. Don explained that the greatest weaknesses in a typical door structure are the door construction itself and the anchoring of the hinges and lock hardware. Most doors are made with hollow-core construction that can be easily broken with a few hard kicks. While solid-core doors are stronger, the stile—the vertical strip of wood at the edge of the door—is still a weak point because it must be drilled to accept the lock hardware.

Most pre-hung doors are also mounted on door jambs made from ¾-inch thick wood. That means the hinges and strike plate for the lock are only supported by that thin piece of wood and are not anchored into the framing structure around the door.

Don's ingenious solution begins with any conventional pre-hung solid-core door. To reinforce the door itself, he uses a router to mill rabbets (grooves) into the stiles of the door. These rabbets accept steel strips are drilled to allow the lock bolt and hinge screws to pass through them. They are then covered with inlaid wood strips to restore the original look of the door.

To reinforce the door frame, Don installs steel plates on the outside of the door jamb. Again, they are carefully drilled to accept the hinge mounting screws and lock hardware.

When the jamb is installed in the doorway, Don uses extra-long steel screws that pass through the wood jamb and the steel plates to anchor into the stud structure around the doorway. The hinge halves that anchor to the jamb receive the same treatment, literally anchoring them into the wall structure.

The hinges themselves are also specially

modified. Starting with heavy-duty steel hinges, Don drills additional matching holes into each hinge plate. He screws a hardened steel screw through the hinge plate attached to the jamb and into the door frame. He then trims it to allow about ¾-inch of the shank to extend above the plate. The hinge plate attached to the door has a matching hole into which the screw shank fits when the door is closed. This enhanced version of a "pinned" hinge makes it practically impossible to knock the door off its hinges, even if the hinge pivot pins are removed.

The other side of the door houses the lock hardware, which includes both a high-quality knob lock and a deadbolt lock. The bolts for both of these pass through the steel strip in the edge of the door, greatly reinforcing the union between the locks and the door stile. The deadbolt extends through the wood into the steel plate on the back of the jamb.

With this style of construction, all components of the door, jamb, and hardware are steel reinforced and anchored securely to the framing structure. I have personally tested this construction method using a test door that Don built for the opening episode of season 3 of *The Best Defense*. I kick hard, but even after numerous full-power kicks, the door held strong.

The Next-Best Thing

I realize that everyone doesn't have Don Vaughan on their side to install custom safe-room doors. The next-best thing would be to follow the same do-it-yourself improvements that I described earlier for your front door and other exterior doors. Invest in a solid-core door and mount it with extra-long wood screws that extend through the hinges and jamb into the framing. Leave one screw protruding about ½ inch and cut off the head to create a pinned hinge. On the other side of the door, replace the standard strike plate with a commercial reinforced plate and install it with long screws to anchor it into the framing. Finally, reinforce the

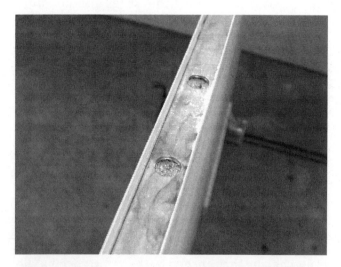

A safe room door must provide a strong barrier to keep home invaders out. This door is being reinforced with steel strips that greatly increase its strength and its connection to the door's surrounding framework.

A high-quality dead bolt lock is also a necessity on a safe room door. This one anchors through the steel strip in the edge of the door and a matching steel strip in the door frame.

lock area of the door with a commercial metal sleeve. These are available at most hardware stores and encase the door and the deadbolt to reinforce its collective structure.

There are also a number of aftermarket door reinforcement kits available online and through major home-improvement realtors. Many of these conveniently ignore some of the more challenging installation details (like the probability that you'll have to trim your door to accommodate their steel reinforcement plates), so don't be fooled by instructions that look too easy to be true. Do your homework and ask questions before you buy. And, just in case, find a good handyman who can come to the rescue if you get in over your head.

Inside the Safe Room

Once you've created your safe room, you need to make sure that you equip it properly. A thoroughly prepared safe room must contain everything you will need to contact the police and explain your emergency, defend yourself if necessary, escape in case of fire, and allow the police entry into your home. The following are the critical items you should have in your safe room to ensure that you can meet all these needs:

- Cell phone and charger: Even if you have a landline phone in your safe room, don't assume that you'll be able to use it during a home invasion. While most criminals won't cut the phone lines the way they do in the movies, they will often take a phone extension off the hook elsewhere in the house to prevent you from calling out. Although it's a good habit to charge your primary cell phone in your safe room, there's no guarantee that it will be there when a sudden home invasion occurs. A better solution is to use your old, out-of-service cell phone. These phones can still be used to dial 911 and can be an important lifesaving tool. By keeping one constantly charging in your safe room, you can ensure you'll always have a usable emergency phone available. Remember, however, that such phones will not have the same caller ID information as a full-service cell phone, so the 911 operator will not know who or where you are. You will have to be able to explain that, which brings us to the next item.

- Written emergency script: You might think that forgetting your name or your address would be impossible, but when you are suffering from the high-level, life-threatening stress of a real home invasion, such things can easily happen. The best way to ensure that you can say everything you need to say in an emergency is to prepare a script in advance. Print it out in large print (easier to see under stress), laminate it, and keep it with your emergency cell phone. This script will "remind" you to explain that you are calling on an emergency cell phone and will provide a clear summary of the situation, your address, your specific location within the house, and the fact that you are armed and in fear for your life. It will also remind you to mention who is with you in the safe room and what you are wearing.

- Firearm, ammunition, and tactical flashlight: Having the ability to defend yourself in the event a home invader makes it through your safe room door is, in my opinion, critical. Doing that effectively typically means having a firearm and the skills to use it. The choice to keep a firearm in the home is one that depends upon many different factors, including your personal beliefs, your spouse's beliefs, the presence and maturity of children in the family, the laws in your area, and many other factors. Evaluating those factors is complicated and beyond the scope of this book. In simple terms, however, you need to accept the fact that anyone who enters your home and is willing to deliver violence to you or your family *will not respond to anything less than more effective and more committed violence.* Once you accept that, ask yourself what gun is most appropriate for use in your home and how you can ensure that it is both quickly available *and* secure from unauthorized access.

- In addition to the gun itself, you need to ensure that you have spare ammunition available and ready to go (a box of ammo and empty magazines isn't good enough). You should also have a high-intensity tactical flashlight and the skill to use it and your firearm together. Again, the tactical use of flashlights is a complicated topic, but at the very least you should understand that threat identification in low-light conditions is critical before you shoot. You should also realize the tactical advantages that you can enjoy by using a light to blind or disorient your attacker and operate more effectively in darkness or diminished light.
- Less-lethal weapon: Even if you live in a state that supports the Castle Doctrine concept, you may find yourself in a situation where you choose not to shoot. At the same time, you have to apply force in some way to persuade an unwelcome person to leave. In that context, a less-lethal weapon like pepper spray—especially a stream, gel, or foam type—can be the key to turning the tables.
- First aid kit: It is possible that you or a family member could suffer an injury on the way to the safe room. Having a well-stocked first aid kit as part of your safe room resources is therefore a very good idea.
- House keys attached to a chemical light stick: When the police arrive, you want them to be able to enter the house and ensure that it is safe before you leave the sanctity of your safe room. The easiest way to do this is to have an extra set of house keys that you can throw out a window to them. Obviously, you would only do this once you have visually confirmed that they are on site. The light stick allows the keys to be found easily in darkness or if you accidentally throw them into the grass or bushes.
- Fire escape ladder: Part of planning your safe room should be anticipating the very worst case scenario. Let's say someone invades your home and you make it successfully to your safe room. Frustrated that he couldn't get to you, he sets the house on fire. You must still have the ability to escape from your safe room without having to open the hallway door—especially if your safe room is on the second floor. An

A safe room should be equipped with a fully charged cell phone, a less-lethal weapon like pepper spray, a tactical flashlight, and, ideally, a firearm with extra ammunition. A written script to guide your call to 911 is also useful to ensure that you remember to include all the necessary information in your statement and don't lock up under stress.

escape window and, if necessary, an escape ladder should therefore also be part of your plan.

Cover, Fields of Fire, and Backstops

One often overlooked aspect of planning a safe room is the consideration and planning of fields of fire. Basically, this comes down to three elements: having some type of cover for yourself and your family, being able to deliver fire at the doorway and entrance area from that cover, and having a solid backstop behind the area you'll be shooting into.

Cover, as you may already know, is something that will actually stop incoming gunfire. Assuming the worst-case scenario—that the home invader is armed with a firearm and shoots through the door or wall—you need to put yourself and your family behind something that is solid enough to have a good chance of stopping a bullet. Unfortunately, the number of things that really qualify as cover in the average home is very limited. Typical interior wall construction—drywall and two-by-fours—won't stop even minor-caliber handgun rounds. Similarly beds, mattresses, dressers, and most of the other stuff found in a typical bedroom won't do much either. Your best bet is to strategically place something that constitutes real cover in your safe room. And the best choices for that are either a large bookcase full of books or a serious gun safe.

Books—especially large hardcover books—make very effective bullet stops. A case full of them therefore makes pretty good cover. Note that books work best when bullets strike them on the flat, not the edge. Therefore, angling the bookshelf to the likely line of fire is more effective than hiding behind it and allowing rounds to hit the books on the spine.

Since part of the goal of a safe room is secure storage of defensive firearms, having a gun safe in that room makes very good sense. If you invest in one that is of substantial construction, it makes even more sense because you can have it do double duty as a source of cover. A full-size

The structure of most homes doesn't offer much in the way of cover against hostile gunfire. A gun safe not only provides safe storage of your firearms, but can also be an excellent source of real cover.

steel gun safe with an open door can literally provide enough cover for you, your spouse, and a couple of kids and makes a great "centerpiece" for your safe room defense strategy.

The next two elements of safe room planning—fields of fire and solid backstops—go hand in hand and should be planned together. To do this, think about firing rounds from various locations in your safe room toward the doorway. Now look beyond the door area and figure out where those rounds would go if they went through your attacker or missed him entirely. As you do this, take into consideration vertical angles as well. If you are kneeling behind cover and shooting at a slight upward angle, how does that affect what the bullet might hit?

The goal of this process is to determine angles of fire that allow you to shoot effectively *and* ensure that any rounds that don't come to rest in your attacker come to rest in something appropriate. If you have a brick home, you are literally surrounded by a solid backstop. All you need to do is to plan your angles to avoid windows. If your home is not entirely made of brick, your choices for solid backstops would be things like fireplaces, brick facades, or—you guessed it—strategically placed bookcases behind the doorway.

When considering angles and fields of fire, you should also think about the potential offered by features like staircases and split levels. Any time that you can shoot at a significant downward angle, you can use the floor (assuming that it is of appropriate construction) as a solid backstop. If you are on a lower level and can target an intruder as he comes down a flight of stairs, the stairs may serve as an effective backstop. Think in three dimensions and plan your angles well. If necessary, use a laser pointer to help visualize your fields of fire and your likely impact points.

Once you've determined the best angles of fire, arrange your bedroom to position your safe or other hard cover at your preferred firing point. This may require some experimentation—and some negotiation with your better half—but it's well worth the effort.

If you plan to use a gun for home defense, you must plan your fields of fire and ensure that you have solid backstops in case your rounds miss or overpenetrate. Shooting at a downward angle from the top of a stairwell not only creates a "choke point" for the attacker, it uses the floor as a good backstop.

CHAPTER 3: HOME INVASIONS

According to a report by the United States Department of Justice, 38% of assaults and 60% of rapes occur during home invasions. Although home invasion is not defined as a specific crime in many states, as a criminal practice, it is becoming increasingly prevalent. Previously, businesses, banks, and similar commercial institutions were the targets of choice for criminals because they held the promise of bigger payoffs. However, as security measures at these businesses have improved, targeting them has gotten increasingly difficult. This has made family homes a very attractive alternative for criminals.

While most people would like to believe that the solution to a home invasion is just a 911 call away, it's not that easy. According to research done by the *Atlanta Journal Constitution* on police response times in major metropolitan areas, it typically takes at least 10 minutes for police to respond to a high-priority emergency call. Atlanta, which had the slowest response time of the seven cities studied, took on average 11 minutes and 12 seconds from the time a high-priority 911 call was received until a police officer arrived at the scene. A lot of bad things can happen to you and your family in 11 minutes. Even worse things can happen if you never have the opportunity to make that call.

While increasing the physical security of your home is definitely worth the effort, it's not an absolute guarantee that you won't be the target of a home invasion. And even if you do have a well-planned safe room, if that invasion occurs when you are in another part of the house, you must either fight your way to the safe room or defend yourself where you are.

Improvised Weapons in the Home and Staging Weapons

The best way to develop sound home invasion reaction plans is to think about different scenarios in advance and address them based on different starting positions in your home. Again, your goal is to keep yourself and your family safe, either by getting to a safe room or fleeing the house to safety. Even if you and your family members are quick and agile, simply outrunning the home invaders may not be enough. You may have to literally fight your way to an exit or your safe room. And to do that, you should consider staging weapons at other locations in your house.

Staged weapons are purpose-designed or improvised weapons that you either preposition in strategic locations in your home or at least mentally acknowledge as part of your planning process. The first step in this process should be to evaluate your family's level of comfort and responsibility with purpose-designed weapons and determine whether they are a good choice. If you and your spouse are both comfortable and competent with firearms, having several handguns or shoulder weapons staged around the house makes perfect sense. If you have small children, obviously that is not a good idea unless they are properly secured against unauthorized access. There are a variety of security devices available for this, ranging from simple trigger locks to biometric safes. Your choice will depend upon the age and maturity of your family members, the layout of your home, and other dynamic factors.

One brilliantly simple method of storing a firearm so it is readily available is a FAST Holster. A FAST Holster isn't really a holster in the traditional sense, but a small platform loaded with powerful rare-earth magnets. These magnets are strong enough to hold a firearm securely, while still allowing it to be quickly removed and brought into action. Rubber coated so they won't mar the finish of your gun, FAST holsters are available in a pistol version and a long-gun version, each containing the appropriate number of magnets for that class of gun.

FAST holsters mount with two screws (included) and can be positioned almost anywhere. Any spot that is normally out of sight but easily reached—like interior closet walls, ceilings, cabinets, under shelves, and the classic under-the-desk mount—works well.

The magnets in FAST holsters are incredibly strong, so all you need is a little bit of available steel to make them work. As such, guns like alloy-framed revolvers can still be suspended by their cylinder and Glocks can be hung from their slides. Despite their strength, removal of the guns from FAST holsters is not difficult and is arguably faster than any other hard-mount method since so much of the gun is exposed. The "draw" is also not restricted to a particular direction, like a traditional holster.

If it is not practical (or affordable) for you to stage firearms around your home, you should consider other types of purpose-designed or improvised weapons. During that process, remember that a good home-defense weapon should be easily accessible, capable of causing serious damage to an attacker, easy to wield, and appropriate to the environmental constraints of your house. The latter point is particularly

If it's safe and practical for you to pre-position firearms around your home, you should consider the FAST holster. It's a rubberized plate that contains powerful magnets and can be used to mount a gun to virtually any flat surface. They are available for both handguns (above) and long guns (opposite page).

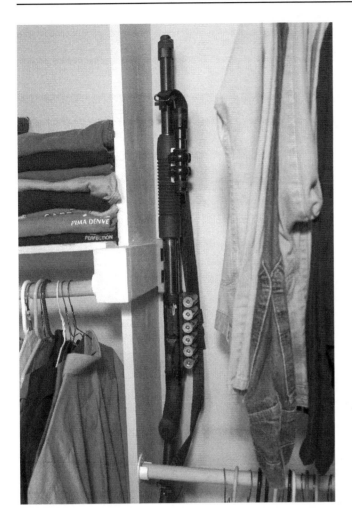

important and often overlooked. To put it simply, it's hard to swing a baseball bat or a golf club in a hallway, so you need to choose a weapon that fits your environment or adapt the skills you use to wield that weapon to the constraints of that environment.

The basic goal of staging weapons should be to create an environment so that no matter where you are in your home, you are never more than a few steps away from an object with serious weapon attributes. Here are just a few examples of the possible types of staged weapons you can have in your home:

- Environmental improvised weapons – Objects that already exist in your home environment that you can easily grab and apply as weapons, such as kitchen knives, frying pans, hammers, screwdrivers, brooms/mops/mop handles, etc.
- Pre-positioned less-lethal weapons – Purpose-designed weapons that offer significant defensive potential but would be difficult to apply with lethal force. Examples include sticks/canes in umbrella stands, pepper spray staged in appropriate places (clipped or secured with Velcro® above doorways), and hardwood dowel security bars in window and sliding door tracks.
- Openly displayed "decorative" weapons – Purpose-designed weapons that are hung for decorative purposes, but can easily be put into use as defensive tools. These could include swords, spears, martial arts weapons and even firearms. Make sure that you plan the placement of these weapons carefully so they arm you, not the home invader, and that they are appropriate to the physical constraints of that part of the house. They should also not be accessible to children or other unauthorized or unqualified users.

Remember that the goal of staging weapons is to give you an immediately accessible tool that increases your ability to fight your way to an exit or the safe room. Depending upon your family composition, you may also use a weapon to fight a delaying or guarding action to "hold off" home invaders while your family members flee to safety. If this is part of your home defense plan, make sure that you use the physical layout of your home to your advantage. Natural choke points like doorways, hallways, and stairwells can be an excellent place to "make a stand," since they funnel the invaders into a confined area. In such situations, long, two-handed thrusting weapons like spears, brooms, sticks, and canes can give you a great advantage if employed properly. The details of the tactics to do this are addressed later in this book in the chapter on self-defense with a cane or walking stick. They are demonstrated with a cane, but are readily adaptable to any similar object.

You should also make a habit of stashing a

weapon in every bathroom as well, or at least realizing that the handle of a plunger or the bar from a towel rack can be used as an improvised weapon. If someone gets into your home when you are using the bathroom (Murphy's Law) or if you are taken hostage in your own home, access to a bathroom will also guarantee access to a weapon.

Finally, to ensure that you can put your home-defense plan into action when you need it, you need to review it and practice often. When it comes to the use of weapons as part of your overall plan, you should quiz and remind yourself often of the locations of your "go-to" weapons in different parts of the house. Practice grabbing a weapon and maneuvering or fighting to exits and safe rooms while "collecting" family members and moving them ahead of you. Identify projectile weapons that you can throw to cover your retreat (anything that you can grab and throw easily and will make an attacker duck and cover—at least for a moment). Practice your verbal commands and remind other family members of their meanings and what they need to do when they hear them.

Your best defense at home should be a careful combination of physical security, sound planning, and well-practiced skills. Do this and your home *will* be your castle.

CHAPTER 4: AWARENESS, AVOIDANCE, DE-ESCALATION AND BOUNDARY SETTING

When most people think of personal protection training, they think of developing hard skills, like learning how to shoot or learning how to fight. But when it comes to actually keeping yourself and your family safe, there's a lot more you need to know. A truly comprehensive personal protection plan should consist of many different layers of defense. And anyone trying to get to you should have to dig through layer after layer of these defenses before you ever get to the point that you have to use any kind of physical skill or draw a weapon. The outer layers of this system are actually the most important, because they represent the skills that you should be applying every day. They include "softer" skills, like awareness, avoidance, de-escalation, and boundary setting.

Awareness

Awareness is a term heard a lot in self-defense training. Everyone knows you're supposed to be aware of your surroundings and look for signs of trouble before it happens, but what does it really mean to be "aware" and what are you supposed to be aware of?

After years of teaching self-defense, the best analogy that I've come up with that allows people to easily understand "active awareness" is to have them think of driving in heavy traffic. When you are driving in heavy traffic, you are actually focused on the task at hand. You're not paranoid; you're not freaking out; but you are actually actively aware of what's going on around you and you are prepared to react. If another car suddenly changes lanes or cuts you off, you're ready to respond with an appropriate action. You are also using all your resources, including your rear-view mirror and side mirrors, to maintain full 360-degree alertness. This attitude and mindset is exactly what you should strive to develop and maintain any time that you are out in public. Yes, it requires work; but it pays big dividends when it comes to keeping yourself safe.

Based on that definition of awareness, the next thing you need to understand is what exactly you are supposed to be looking for. Well, in technical terms, they are known as "pre-incident indicators." In laymen's terms, it's basically any action or behavior that might give you a hint that someone is trying to size you up as a victim. Some specific examples of this might

include:
- One or more people loitering at a choke point or likely ambush site
- One or more people coordinating their movement with yours
- Predatory behavior, like circling or blocking your route
- People looking around unnaturally or trading looks as you approach
- "Grooming" actions like smoothing one's hair to try to look casual
- Weight shifting or "winding up" in preparation for a strike
- Hard looks at what you are wearing or carrying
- Any physical bump or nudge
- Verbal challenges
- Conversations initiated by strangers
- Vehicles following you or making more than one pass
- Anyone hiding his hand or hands behind his leg or back or in a jacket pocket
- Unnatural hand positions that suggest that someone might be "palming" something—like a weapon (natural hand positions typically have extended thumbs)
- Any "gut" feeling or instinct that tells you something is not right

Avoidance

What do you do if you notice one of the above indicators? Basically, you implement the second layer of our defensive system: avoidance. Avoidance is a commitment to NOT putting yourself at risk or becoming involved in an incident if you can possibly avoid it. Although that may sound obvious, many victims of crimes later comment that they "knew something was wrong, but kept going anyway." Don't let that happen to you!

At the very least, anytime that you suspect that *anything* is out of the ordinary, stop. By simply stopping and observing, you change the dynamics of that situation and you send a very strong message to anyone that might be sizing you up. They now realize that you are aware of your surroundings and suspect a potential threat. That means that you are much less desirable as a victim—which is exactly what you want!

Changing the dynamics of your situation is also a powerful way of exercising avoidance. If you are uncomfortable with someone who appears to be walking toward you on an intercepting path, casually change your direction so you put some type of obstacle between you (a park bench, trees, cars, etc.) and remain aware of that person without staring or fixating.

One of the many specific signs of potential trouble is when unknown people coordinate their movement with you and/or each other. The coordinated movement of these three men should be cause for serious concern.

Awareness, Avoidance, De-escalation and Boundary Setting

One important note when it comes to looking at a suspected threat: Do not establish hard eye contact. People are fond of the cliché "The eyes are the window to the soul" and believe that looking into someone's eyes will reveal their intent. Unfortunately, in modern street culture a hard look can be interpreted as a challenge or a sign of disrespect. That act alone can provoke an incident instead of avoiding one.

So where do you look when you look at a person? I recommend looking at the chest. This puts your vision below his or her eyes and allows you to easily include elbows and belt line. It's impossible to move your arm to attack without first moving your elbow, so elbow movement is a great "early warning" indicator. Most weapons are carried somewhere around the belt line, so monitoring it is also a good way to identify signs of trouble early on.

Lowering your head slightly to look at the chest also has the effect of allowing you to see more of the ground around you. That not only helps you maintain spatial awareness of terrain and obstacles around you, it also makes your peripheral vision more effective since you can "see feet" much more easily. The next time you're in a crowd, keep your eyes level and try to get a feel for the number of people around you and their locations and distances. Then lower your gaze to pick up more of the ground around you. You'll find that it's much easier to gauge who's around you and where they are with a slightly lowered line of vision.

You must also learn to trust your instincts. If something doesn't feel right, even if you don't know why, don't walk into that situation. Turn around, go back to a populated, well-lit area, and regroup. If possible, get a group of friends or a security officer to accompany you, but don't put yourself at risk.

De-escalation

De-escalation is probably the hardest defensive skill to learn because it basically means being smarter than your own ego and not giving in to the temptation to prove yourself. That is a difficult task for most people.

You must understand and embrace the fact that there is a huge difference between defending yourself against a true attack and "getting into a fight." If you are truly committed to the idea of avoiding violent conflict, you must avoid *all* situations that could lead to violence. That includes situations where you are morally right and a belligerent troublemaker—even one desperately in need of a lesson in manners—is clearly wrong.

To do this, you need to make the commitment not to fight for stupid reasons. That includes fighting to "prove" anything. Remember, the only time you should have to use physical skills is when you are truly forced to defend yourself and you have no other choice. If someone gets in your face for whatever reason, remain aware of your environment, keep yourself guarded without provoking him, and use your verbal skills to calm the situation. Apologize, tell him he's right (even if he's not), and don't let the situation escalate to violence.

Although this concept may seem distasteful to you, there's a good reason for it: If you choose to fight someone to "teach him a lesson," what you might think will be a fistfight could, to him, be a viable reason for a stabbing or a shooting. The world has changed and many people out there—especially those in desperate need of an ass kicking—just don't play by your rules or share your sense of fairness.

I grew up in an era where kids got into fights. If someone got out of line or pushed another kid too hard, a fight would ensue and some form of balance would be achieved. In most cases, this was a good thing because nature typically ensured that troublemakers would eventually run into someone tougher and more capable who would put them in their proper place—recumbent, bleeding, and humbled.

Now that we live in a "kinder, gentler" world, fighting in schools is no longer tolerated. Instead of a natural system of checks and balances that tends to promote personal accountability, the "appropriate" response seems to be to allow things to build up to the point that shootings and stabbings take the place of schoolyard fistfights. As that type of mindset becomes more prevalent, the world becomes more dangerous. You need to know that and remember that the best revenge is living well. You can't un-stupid people and you can't single-handedly teach the world manners, so focus on keeping yourself and your family safe.

If you're still not convinced that de-escalation is a worthwhile tactic, bear in mind that some criminals will use any kind of minor conflict they can generate as "bait" to draw you into a situation. While you are focused on the fistfight that will teach him a lesson, you are not paying attention to his three friends that just walked up behind you to stomp you to death. Don't take the bait! Avoidance equals winning.

Boundary Setting

The final non-physical "layer" of your defense should be boundary setting. Just like it sounds, it is the art of establishing boundaries between you and a potential threat that allow you to maintain distance. Distance is what allows reaction time, so maintaining it should always be a priority in keeping yourself safe.

Boundary setting is a combination of verbal and visual communication that sends a clear message that you are not going to play by the attacker's rules. In the process, you establish a clear boundary between yourself and your attacker so he understands you do not want him to approach you.

Setting boundaries is a critically important skill because many criminals will "interview" you verbally before they attack to determine your willingness to resist. If your reaction—or lack thereof—leads them to believe that your guard is down and that it is safe for them to close the distance, they will. And the closer they get, the faster they can move on you and the fewer options you have to stop them.

Good boundary setting skills should communicate clearly that you are not going to play the other person's game and that you will maintain distance between you. At the same time, your skills should be appropriate to the level of the confrontation and should not escalate it or provoke an attack. To achieve this balance, you need several graduated levels of response.

The lowest level of boundary setting consists of "pat" responses that you can deliver instantly and confidently to any type of approach. If a stranger approaches you on the street for any reason, do not answer questions or get sucked into a conversation. A short, confident "No thanks" and "Sorry, I can't help you" will cover most situations. If you punctuate this with a single, upraised hand (not a "wave," but a subtle "stay back" gesture), you make it clear that you are not going to play by his rules.

If the stranger continues his approach, repeat your pat response a little more sternly and make solid visual contact with his chest. Again, the reason you look at his chest is to clearly acknowledge him while avoiding any eye contact issues that may be interpreted as a challenge or form of disrespect. It gives you a specific place to look that also allows you to see the position and status of his hands. Since most people cannot attack without some type of preparatory movement of the shoulders or elbows, you are also primed to "read" any potentially hostile actions.

If your initial response does not have the desired effect or if you feel threatened, try to position yourself to place any available obstacles (bench, car, lamppost, etc.) between you and the stranger. Functionally, this increases the distance between you because he has to go around or over the obstacle to get to you. At the same time, you should progress to the next level of verbalization by advising him to "Stay back." The tone of this command can be varied to match the intensity of the confrontation, but stick with the phrase "Stay back." The advantage of this is that you are subtly telling him to do what he is *already* doing. Psychologically, it's a standoff and nobody wins or loses.

If he still doesn't comply and tries to

Awareness, Avoidance, De-escalation and Boundary Setting

approach closer, it's time to up the ante and take positive control of the situation. At that point, your tone of voice should escalate to a loud, authoritative "Back off!" If appropriate, you can also use the phrase "Show me your hands!" if you can't see them and suspect that he might have a weapon. As you do this, you should also assume a "ready" stance, with your hands open and up with your fingertips roughly level with your eyes. Your stance should be offset, so your weak side is forward and your strong side back. This will place your weak hand in front and your strong hand slightly behind it, with both hands naturally on your body's centerline in front of your face. Don't "blade" or angle yourself too far, however, and keep your hips and shoulders squared up with the threat.

The "ready" stance is consistent with the human body's natural reactions to a potentially violent threat. It also provides the readiness and functionality of a true fighting stance without overtly provoking anyone. The raised hands not only punctuate the message to back off, but they also immediately establish you as the "good guy" to any witnesses in the area.

A Continuum...Of Sorts

Awareness, avoidance, de-escalation, and boundary setting are explained here as a continuum—a logical progression from one "layer" to the next. However, in the dynamics of a real situation, you may not have the opportunity to progress through them in order. Although you should always strive to be aware and avoidant, if you fail to recognize a potential threat until the situation has "evolved" too far, you may find yourself progressing immediately to boundary setting. Similarly, for some situations de-escalation might be appropriate, while others might demand an immediate jump to boundary setting.

It is important to understand and master all the tools you have available to you, while at the same time remaining adaptable enough to apply the right tools at the right time.

The ready position is not overtly aggressive, yet it sets strong boundaries and gets your hands up and ready to react.

CHAPTER 5:
EMPTY-HAND TACTICS

The tools and tactics of awareness, avoidance, de-escalation, and boundary setting detailed in the previous chapter should provide the outer layers of your personal defense system. They should also inspire you to devote significant planning and training time to mastering these skills and making them your first choice as a "go-to" defensive response.

But no matter how committed you are to recognizing and avoiding trouble, "it" can still happen to you. Despite your best efforts, you may still find yourself in a situation where non-physical skills are simply not enough. And when "it" happens, the best—and only—tool for the job is committed, ruthlessly effective violence. To that end, there are a few things you need to understand, internalize, and remember.

First, you have already exhausted the "conversational aspects" of your relationship with this person (or people). You have given him fair warning that you do not want to play his game and that your safety is more important than his plans for you. With that clear, understanding the sociological aspects of how he became what he is or why he's choosing to commit a crime are totally irrelevant. His disadvantaged upbringing, the socio-economic climate of his neighborhood, and any other details of his socialization process must all take a back seat to the fact that he is planning on hurting you to either take your possessions, make you do something repugnant for, to, or with him, or just because he happens to like hurting people. Accept that and focus on the task at hand.

Speaking of the task at hand, remember that your primary goal is always to achieve safe escape. You're not out to prove anything except that you want to get out of that situation as quickly and safely as possible. If a quick finger jab to his eyes creates that opportunity, go for it. You do not need to throw him to the ground and apply a submission hold to "win" that encounter. Winning is all about getting away safely.

With that in mind, make sure that your training emphasizes the concept of what we call "mobility kills"—tactics that have serious detrimental effect on an attacker's ability to stand, walk, and run. If you can render him immobile, you have a much better chance of escaping safely. Powerful, direct attacks to the ankles, shins, and knees work great for this purpose, but remember that impairing his vision also prevents him from running effectively, so don't forget the power of eye strikes.

Committed, effective, skillful violence is a righteous tool in your personal protection arsenal. When you need it, you *really* need it, so make the decision and the commitment to use it when necessary.

Practical Empty-Hand Skills

The starting point of my approach to empty-hand skills is the same as the starting point of the de-escalation and boundary-setting skills discussed earlier: the basic ready stance. Whether you are reacting to a sudden threat or stimulus (a "startle response") or an escalating situation, the ready stance offers all the attributes you need to protect yourself and react quickly and efficiently.

In the ready stance, your feet are spread about shoulder width apart and slightly staggered to provide a good base. Consistent with human instinctive reactions to a violent threat, your knees will be bent, and your hands will be raised to about shoulder level. Your weak hand should be slightly in front of your strong hand and both hands should be open, palms forward, and in front of your face. Do not "bracket" your head, but instead keep your hands in front of you—almost like a boxer's guard. Again, consistent with instinct, your shoulders will be slightly hunched and your chin tucked.

The ready position provides all the attributes of a true fighting stance without looking overtly offensive or provocative. In fact, the position of the open palms serves as a universal sign language to "Stop. Stay Back." It also clearly communicates to any witnesses that you were the one defending yourself.

By keeping your hands on your centerline—in front of your face—you not only protect your head but you also motivate your attacker to swing wide. As strange as it may seem, most people will not punch through your hands and will try to go around your guard. The wider they swing, the slower they are and the easier it is to "read" your attacker's strike and know what you're defending against. In simple terms, you use the tip of your lead-hand middle finger as a front sight. For example, if you are right handed, you would have your left hand in front of your right and your left middle finger would define your centerline.

If your attacker's fist (or other weapon) approaches from the left of your centerline (based on your perspective), your defense will be oriented to the left of your centerline. If you the fist or weapon approaches to the right of your centerline, your defense will go to the right. If he attacks straight down centerline, you will slap his attack downward and then sweep it to one side. More on all this later...

Have a Plan and Work Your Plan

Most traditional martial arts require students to memorize many different defensive techniques that are specific to individual attacks. In most cases, you also have to learn the techniques on both the left and right sides. In a real, spontaneous attack, you not only have to react to a sudden stimulus, you also have to search through a long list of possible responses before you choose and hopefully apply the right one. Simple logic dictates that the more you have to learn, the longer it will take to get good at it.

My approach to the problem is very different and can be summed up by the phrase, "Have a plan and work your plan." What that means is that we strive to develop a set of simple, gross-motor movements that are not only easy to learn and apply, but they also serve multiple functions depending upon the changing dynamics of the situation. In this way, no matter how the situation evolves, you just need to keep doing what you're doing and it will get the job done.

My approach also takes advantage of your natural athleticism and instinctive gross motor skills. If you are naturally right handed, you hit harder with your right hand. Rather than trying to train your left hand to catch up to the right, it's much easier to focus on hitting with your right hand whenever possible. The "plan" that I teach for doing this starts with a basic combination.

Empty-hand Tactics

Starting from the ready stance (assuming a left-forward stance, since most people are right handed), our basic combination begins by extending the left palm straight forward. There is no "wind up" or telegraphing—it just shoots straight forward. The next action is a natural downward palm strike with the right hand, much like the action of serving a volleyball. This strike goes to the spot in space previously occupied by the left palm, which naturally retracts as the right hand swings. The right-hand strike is followed by another extension of the left palm, and another right-hand palm strike or, alternately, a right hammerfist strike—hitting with the soft bottom of the closed fist. This sequence may be repeated as many times as necessary and constitutes the basic tactic of "cycling"—a term borrowed from my friend Kelly McCann, one of the premier close-combat instructors in the business.

Although cycling may seem deceptively simple, it can actually have many different functions—both offensive and defensive. To understand this, let's first consider the possible functions of the left hand. At the lowest functional level, the extension of the left palm is just a feint to draw your attacker's attention away from the real strike with the right hand. It can also be used like a boxer's jab to either strike the face or simply obscure the attacker's vision, increasing the chances of a successful power strike with the right hand. By straightening your wrist, the left palm strike can easily become a finger jab, targeting the eyes or throat. If your attacker has a guard up, the left hand can be used to slap his guard aside or pin it to his body to create an opening to strike with your other hand. It can also be a simple opening strike—either hard or soft—that allows you to gauge distance and "index" your target spatially. Once your left hand touches something and knows where it is in space, your right hand can accurately hit to that same spot—fighting by Braille.

Defensively, the extension of the left palm can be a check or a stop that stops or at least interrupts the power of an attacker's strike. Typically this works best against his bicep or shoulder when he swings wide. It can also be an "off ramp"—a deflection that takes an attacker's punch off target and redirects it down your arm into your armpit. Your extended palm can also wrap, grab, or control your attacker's head or arm to stabilize him for the power hit.

In learning cycling, it is important to understand that the right hand strike is purposely done at a downward angle rather than a straight, punch-like action. The reason for this is two-fold. First, hammer-like strikes are more consistent with the gross motor skills that will take over under stress, so it's best to stick with what you know you will do instinctively. Secondly, striking down on your attacker's nose, cheekbone, ear, neck, or collarbone makes it less likely that your hand will hit his teeth. And in today's world, that's a major concern. To put it simply, the last thing you want to do is to "win" a street encounter, only to die of AIDS or Hepatitis a few years later because you let your attacker's teeth break your skin.

The downward, elliptical motion of the power hand in cycling also provides multiple functions in addition to effective, rapid-fire hitting. Let's say your attacker takes exception to being hit and blocks your palm or hammerfist attack with his arm. By simply continuing the elliptical motion of the strike and hooking his blocking hand as you re-chamber you can easily "clear" his block, removing that barrier. As you do, your left hand naturally extends again to strike, check, or grab. Your right hand is then quickly back on target for more hits.

Similarly, if your attacker grabs your right wrist to try to stop you from hitting, the leverage inherent in cycling's elliptical motion is all you need to break free. Simply continue the cycling movement and pull the attacker's hand toward you as you chamber for another strike. Your hand will naturally lever downward, breaking his grip and pulling him in close for another hit. Again, as you do this, your left hand will be actively striking, gouging, checking, grabbing, or just physically indexing the target to let your right hand know where to hit next.

Although cycling provides a tremendously powerful and versatile striking tool, it alone is not enough to ensure your ability to escape safely. Another excellent empty-hand tool—and the next movement in the basic combination—is an elbow strike. The horizontal elbow combines the explosive rotation of the hips with a fast, loose whipping action of the shoulder to generate tremendous speed and power. By keeping your hand open and loose, you avoid any unnecessary muscle tension that would hinder the strike. The striking area is the last few inches of hard, flat bone near the point of the elbow—an area with few nerves that enables you to hit full force without fear of injury.

Like all our other empty-hand tools, the mechanics of the elbow strike are not limited to striking actions only. They also provide perfect leverage for escaping from any type of wrist grab an attacker might attempt. When he grabs, rather than a fancy technique, simply throw a horizontal elbow. The powerful mechanics of the motion will lever your wrist right out of his grasp. Follow with a few rounds of cycling and a solid kick to the shin and your technique creates itself.

Striking with the horizontal elbow is a powerful rotational movement. At the completion of it, your shoulders and hips should be rotated and your core muscles taut. In this position, you are naturally chambered for the next movement of the combination: a right knee strike. Although the groin is a natural and desirable target for this strike, don't hold back if it's not accessible—just fire. Whether you hit bladder, quadriceps muscle, femoral nerve, or the common peroneal nerve on the outside of the thigh, you will still hit with powerful effect.

When you throw the knee strike, you should back it with the entire force of your body and literally "walk" forward into it. Do NOT hit and retract. By practicing to step forward, you learn to always strike with full body commitment. Very importantly, you also learn how to maintain your balance if your knee strike misses or skips off the target. By stepping down, you also learn to harness the final movement of the combination: a stomping kick and/or foot trap.

As I've mentioned previously, the ultimate goal of all self-defense is your safe escape. And one of the best ways to create that opportunity with unarmed fighting skills is with a "mobility kill"—a powerful attack that literally destroys your attacker's ability to stand, walk, or run. This "big gun" tactic is best delivered with your most powerful body weapons, your legs, in the form of a stomp kick aimed directly at your attacker's knee, shin, or ankle.

While kicks to the knee can certainly cause devastating damage to the joint and are an excellent way of decisively stopping an attacker, they are sometimes difficult to land cleanly. Delivered from the front, they often skid off the pointed surface of the bent knee. That's why I prefer kicks to the shin and ankle instead. Not only is the surface area of the target larger and easier to hit, but rolling an attacker's ankle with a full-power kick is one of the best high-probability, low-risk tactics you can imagine. By setting it up with several repetitions of cycling to get your attacker's attention up high, you can often create an ideal opportunity for a fight-stopping low-line kick that he will never see coming.

Once you've developed a feel for cycling, the elbow strike, knee strikes, and low-line stomps, practice connecting them in a fluid sequence. Start with a single or multiple left-right cycling motion. When appropriate, close the distance and replace your right hand strike with a right horizontal elbow. Using the powerful hip turn that generated the elbow as a spring load, fire a right knee strike and/or low-line stomp. At the conclusion of the right stomp, step down and be prepared to follow with a left knee or stomp if necessary. This full combination is incredibly versatile and forms the foundation of a basic, yet very sound empty-hand personal defense system. The flow of the sequence can—and should—be adjusted to repeat or delete individual strikes based on the dynamics of the situation and the reactions of the person you're hitting. The following photo sequences show several examples of how this powerful combination can be applied to defend against a variety of common street attacks.

The core of the author's empty-hand system of self-defense is a multi-purpose sequence of movements that includes "cycling," a horizontal elbow strike, a knee, a kick, and a foot trap. By exploring the "physiological potential" of this sequence, it can be used to defend against a wide range of attacks.

The Best Defense

This sequence illustrates the preemptive use of the basic sequence. When an attacker draws back to punch, the defender strikes to the face with his left palm, obscuring the attacker's vision and leaving him open for the right palm strike to the ear. Another left palm keeps the attacker off balance and sets him up for the right elbow strike, followed immediately by a right knee to the thigh and—continuing the same forward drive—a right kick to the ankle.

Empty-hand self-defense tactics don't need to be complicated to be effective. You also don't need months or years of martial arts training to develop usable skills. By focusing on natural gross-motor movements that are consistent with the body's reactions to stress, emphasizing the dominant side of your body to develop maximum power, and learning to apply a few basic movements to defend against a broad range of circumstances, you can develop potent fighting skills in very short order. In short, have a plan, and work your plan.

For detailed instruction on my system of empty-hand self-defense, please look into my Practical Unarmed Combatives video series, available from Stay Safe Media (www.staysafemedia.com).

Empty-hand Tactics

Here the same sequence is used defensively against a punch. When the attacker throws a right punch, the defender extends his left palm between the attacker's fist and head, creating an "off ramp" for the punch. The defender then uses his downward strike to check and pin the attacker's left hand. The action of the second left palm traps the attacker's left hand against his chest, leaving him helpless against the right horizontal elbow and right knee strike.

The Best Defense

CHAPTER 6: IMPROVISED WEAPONS

The idea of using improvised weapons for personal defense has been around as long as man. In a critical situation, human instinct naturally compels us to grab the closest, sturdiest object and use it to fight for our survival. Due to the events of recent years—particularly the phenomena of active shooters, workplace violence, and school shootings—the carry of purpose-designed weapons has become much more restricted. And with that trend, the number of "non-permissive" environments where weapons are totally forbidden has increased significantly.

History clearly shows that banning weapons has no real effect on stopping violent crimes. Laws only affect the law abiding, so we "good guys" typically only have two choices: either play by the rules and be vulnerable to violent attacks or break the rules and carry a weapon.

Fortunately, there is a third choice. By understanding the how to recognize and use innocuous, everyday objects as improvised weapons, you can bend the rules and ensure that you always have a capable weapon available no matter where you are.

Reality Check

Defending yourself against a committed attack with a purpose-designed weapon is challenging. The less capable your weapon is the tougher that task becomes. With that in mind, the last thing you want to do is to fool yourself into relying on something that doesn't have a high probability of *really* hurting your attacker.

The best way to ensure your safety in a street attack is to quickly and decisively disable your attacker. In simple terms, you must hurt him badly enough to make him stop trying to hurt you. Anything that is not a direct route to achieving this goal is a waste of time, so skip the cheesy MacGuyver tricks. Concentrate on finding and carrying things that you can grab at a moment's notice and swing with full force to create fight-stopping damage. You must also make sure that whatever you grab does not do more harm to you than the bad guy.

For example, many self-defense "experts" recommend the use of keys as an improvised weapon. The methods taught for using them include flailing or raking with the keys or placing them between your fingers to create a "spiked" punch. Think about that. If someone is really intent on hurting you and you slap him across the face with your keys, do you think you'll really inflict enough damage to make him stop? Probably not.

Assume that you're being attacked right now. Pull out your keys and position the three largest, longest ones between your fingers. Go.

How long did that take? If you were actually being attacked, was that a productive use of your time? To really find out, you'd have to try hitting something with your keys between your fingers. You're welcome to try it, but I'll save you the suspense. If you actually hit something hard with keys between your fingers, it hurts—you. You are very likely to injure your fingers. And when you do, you're likely to drop your keys and potentially lose your means of escape.

The self-defense world is full of gimmicks and bullshit. Don't trust your safety to clichés and unproven advice. Learn to think for yourself.

Get Off the Couch

Another critical aspect of using improvised weapons in self-defense is actually investing the time and energy to develop real defensive skills. *Thinking* about stabbing someone with a pen isn't enough; you need to actually practice the skills of doing through challenging, realistic training. Your training should emphasize simple, gross-motor-skill body mechanics that are practical for critical incidents and common to the application of a variety of improvised weapons.

You must also accept the fact that improvised-weapon tactics alone may not be enough to end a fight. A few well-placed strikes with a ballpoint pen will certainly leave a lasting impression; however, they are not guaranteed to make him stop. By using pen tactics to create an opportunity for a true disabling strike—like a low-line kick to the knee or ankle—you have a much more reliable and effective defensive skill set.

If these principles sound familiar to you, they should, because they are exactly the same as the critical elements of the empty-hand tactics discussed in the previous chapter. Those tactics work extremely well without a weapon. If you amp up the hammerfist strike by packing that fist with a sturdy object, those tactics work even better because you can hit harder and cause more damage than with your empty hand alone. Even better, you don't have to learn an entirely new skill set—you simply use what you already know. The less there is to learn and remember, the quicker you develop usable defensive skills and the easier you maintain them. Remember: "Have a plan, and work your plan."

Categories of Improvised Weapons

In my practice and teaching of improvised weapon use, I separate them into three basic categories:

- Prepared Weapons – Items that in their basic form are not capable weapons, but with a little preparation can have weapon potential. For example, a magazine by itself won't do much, but rolled tightly it can be a potent weapon. The "keys-between-the-fingers" trick would also fall into this category—and hammer home the fact that any weapon that requires too much preparation is not practical, especially against a spontaneous attack.
- Weapons of Opportunity – Items that you find in your environment that can be adapted to weapon use, like a rock, beer bottle, a mop, or a trash can lid.
- Personal-Carry Items – Items that you can easily carry on your person that can be used as weapons, like a flashlight or a ballpoint pen.

Weapon Attributes and Awareness

All serious students of self-defense know that "awareness" is a key component of a good personal-defense plan. When most people think of awareness, they think of color-code systems, condition "yellow," and looking for signs of unusual activity that could represent potential threats. All of these aspects of awareness are correct, but real awareness goes much deeper than that. It should include things like assessing your footing and your ability to move quickly, consciousness of obstacles, cover, and concealment, mental planning of escape routes and, very importantly, consciousness of potential improvised weapons in your environment.

Many things can qualify as improvised weapons, but the best objects are those that share a number of common attributes. By learning to identify these attributes—and objects that possess them— and spot them as you move through different environments, you'll greatly expand your defensive options.

The attributes that make a good improvised weapon include:

- Structural integrity/strength – The object must have the integrity to stand up to full-power impact. If it doesn't, you must recognize that limitation and be prepared to back it up with something else.
- Appropriate mass to wield or employ effectively – Objects that are too light don't hit very hard. Very heavy objects cannot be wielded with speed. If possible, look for something that offers a happy medium.
- Offers immediate access and employment – Violent situations happen quickly and very suddenly. Focus on things that you can grab and use very quickly.
- Versatility – Some objects can be used to strike and block. The more the tool can do, the better it will serve you.

While developing your understanding of weapon attributes, you should also be aware of the basic categories of weapons based on the types of damage they can be used to inflict and the types of functions they can perform. These categories include:

- Impact Weapons – Suitable for striking and creating blunt trauma.
- Edged – Suitable for cutting or hacking.
- Pointed – Capable of puncturing or delivering highly focused impact.
- Flexible – Suitable for whipping, entangling, and possibly striking.
- Shield – Capable of blocking or deflecting an attacker's strikes.
- Multi-function – An object that is capable of providing two or more functions.

Weapon Grip

Using an improvised weapon effectively begins with a proper grip. A good grip allows you to strike with full force while managing impact shock and protecting your hand from injury. The three basic grips I teach for improvised weapon use are:

- Hammer grip – Gripping the weapon in your fist like a hammer. This can be used for both small "fist load" weapons and larger stick-like weapons.

A hammer grip is basically making a natural fist around a weapon—like gripping a hammer. You can then swing the weapon or strike with the butt, as shown here.

The Best Defense

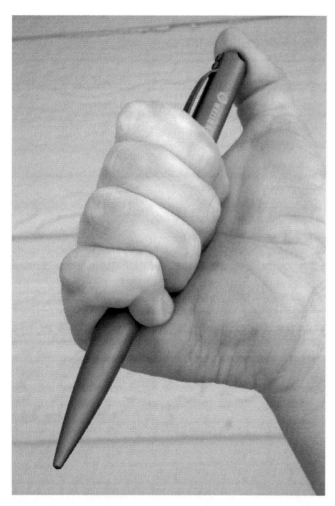

Reverse or "icepick" grip is used for downward or inward hammerfist-style strikes. For maximum power, cap the weapon—here a Tuff-Writer tactical pen—with your thumb to secure the grip.

- Reverse grip – This is basically identical to the hammer grip, but the object extends from the little-finger side of your fist. Also called "icepick grip," it works best with downward or inward hammerfist-style strikes. For maximum strength, cap the top of the weapon with your thumb to lock it into the hand.
- Index-finger grip – Bracing the weapon against your palm and extending your index finger along the length of the weapon. This works well for weapons like pens and allows striking with great accuracy.
- Palm grip – Gripping the object in the palm of your hand, like a ball. This is best for objects that don't fit the fully-closed fist—like rocks, ash trays, and beer mugs.

The Mechanics of Wielding a Weapon

During the stress of a violent encounter, people typically revert to instinct. When it comes to body mechanics, they will most often lead with their weak hand—trying to grab and control with it if possible—while striking with forehand or overhand gross-motor-skill blows with their strong hand. Backhand blows, though less common, usually consist of backhand hammerfist strikes.

Since this is what we will naturally do under stress, it is also the best template for a simple, foolproof skill set—at least for one-handed weapons. Known as "cycling" when performed empty handed, it is a dead-simple method of employing most improvised weapons. If you read the last chapter, it is also something you should already know. Just place a weapon in your dominant hand, make a fist, and do what you already know how to do empty handed. Again, you will use the palm of your left hand to jab, block, check, and move your attacker's limbs out of the way to create openings. The natural "hammering" motion of your right hand enables you to strike hard, fast, and accurately at exposed targets—but now with the extra benefit of a hard object that doesn't feel pain. If you're a lefty, just do the mirror image of what's explained here.

By using the same body mechanics for both empty-hand and improvised-weapon skills, you create a system of tactics that emphasizes "common ground." Functionally, you have less to learn, less to remember, and fewer decisions to make in the stress of an actual defensive situation. Also, if you happen to drop your weapon or it gets "stuck" in your attacker, you don't have to change gears. Let go and just keep hitting.

What do you hit? In simple terms, your attacker. But to be a bit more specific, use hard objects to hit hard things, like the nose, cheekbones, temples, collarbones, sternum,

Improvised Weapons

elbows, and hands. Pointy objects are best applied to soft, vital targets, like the eyes, neck and jugular notch, armpits, and other "tender bits." They can also be targeted at the hands—especially the backs of the hands—to take them out of the fight. If your pointed object penetrates the skin and gets stuck in the target, the pushing or hitting of the left palm that should immediately follow it and the re-chambering motion of your striking hand should allow you to dislodge the weapon and go back to work.

Go Low

Unless you've landed a really telling blow—like a thrust to the eye—after you've struck a few times your attacker will try to protect himself and spoil your aim. At that point, switch gears and deliver a low-line kick to the shin, ankle, or knee. The inside of the ankle is particularly favored, since a simple soccer-style kick will roll the ankle painfully, possibly breaking the tibia and almost certainly disabling him so you can get away.

This tactic is extremely important in that it becomes your real source of stopping power. As mentioned previously, the less capable your weapon, the harder it is to physically disable an attacker with it. Rather than trying to finish

The index-finger grip braces one end of the weapon against the palm and guides the striking end with the index finger. A simple poke with your finger can easily become a potent, and extremely accurate, strike with the business end of the weapon.

Large objects like rocks, coffee mugs, etc. are best held in a palm grip. The natural striking motion is similar to throwing a ball.

the fight with a salt shaker or a ballpoint pen, use that object to deliver some telling, possibly debilitating blows that will force your attacker to raise his hands to protect himself. Then, as soon as the opportunity presents itself, deliver a powerful low-line kick to destroy his mobility and create what you really want: an opportunity to escape.

Training to deliver this low-line kick should be an integral part of your improvised-weapons practice. A good way to do this is to roll up a rubber-backed rug or a bamboo area mat and tape it with duct tape to create a resilient "leg." Have a partner hold it and practice "kicking and sticking" to dump your entire body weight into the blow.

This same target also makes a handy tool for practicing strikes with various improvised weapons. Taking the time to actually hit something with your tactical pen, flashlight, and a variety of common objects that you might find in your environment is critical because it allows you to actually "feel" what it's like to hit. This experience will not only help you develop skill, accuracy, and the confidence to use the tactic in a fight, it also helps you find "hot spots" on various objects—protruding surfaces that might do you more harm than good. Finding this out now is much better than disabling your own hand in the middle of a critical incident.

Even if you do carry a purpose-designed weapon, improvised weapons can be a great adjunct to your tactics. Make a habit of having a pen, flashlight, or other improvised weapon in your hand and ready to go when you're out on the street. In this way, you can literally walk down the street "armed" without raising any eyebrows. If a situation does arise, use the improvised weapon as a line of first defense and then use the time and distance you've created to transition to your purpose-designed weapon.

Used properly, improvised weapons can be everything from a powerful last resort to a purposeful first choice. By learning to identify and assess them as part of your overall awareness and employ them effectively with a solid, basic skill set, you can ensure that you'll be "forever armed."

One of the greatest advantages of improvised weapons like tactical pens is that they can be carried in the hand in public without attracting any attention.

CHAPTER 7: FLASHLIGHT TACTICS

When most people think of flashlight tactics, they think of the application of the light in conjunction with a handgun. But just as the gun is not a cure-all for all self-protection needs, the potential of the flashlight as a personal-protection tool is also much broader than just a headlight for a gun.

A good flashlight offers many advantages as a personal-defense tool. In the simplest sense, it allows you to see in the dark—a function that takes away the bad guy's advantage of concealment. It also greatly expands your awareness because it reminds you to look around and motivates you to be alert in diminished light.

A flashlight makes an excellent striking weapon, providing all the same function as a kubotan or yawara stick, in a much more innocuous and "PC" package.

Best of all, a good, bright flashlight can be used as a force-multiplier, blinding and momentarily disorienting an attacker to either create an opening for a strike or an opportunity to escape.

Attributes of a Tactical Flashlight

Although the buzz word "tactical" is so overused it has lost much of its meaning, the qualifications of a tactical flashlight are actually pretty clear. To really function well in all possible personal-defense applications, it needs to have the following attributes:

- At least a 65-lumen output (brighter is even better) with a pre-focused beam
- An impact-resistant bulb—either an LED or a shock-isolated incandescent bulb
- Solid, high-quality construction that supports its use as an impact weapon
- Ergonomics that allow a solid grip and effective management of impact shock when used as a striking tool
- A large enough size to grasp firmly with at least a half-inch of the light protruding from each side of your fist
- A small enough size to be conveniently carried
- A pocket clip or carrier that allows an immediate access and draw
- A tail-mounted switch that allows momentary actuation of the light

If your light has at least all these features, it qualifies as both a lighting tool and a potent weapon—exactly what you need on the street.

Awareness

The first level of using a flashlight in personal protection is as an awareness tool. Obviously, awareness requires the ability to see. In darkness, or at least diminished lighting conditions—where many attacks occur—that requires light.

By using your light to eliminate shadows and illuminate areas of darkness from a safe distance, you not only identify potential threats before you get close to them, you also let the world know that you are alert and actively aware of your surroundings. As we've discussed previously, that "hard-target" appearance is a powerful deterrent in and of itself. Most importantly, if you can train yourself to draw your flashlight and use it to look for potential threats, you are effectively training yourself to be aware. The light is both a tool and a physical reminder to be actively aware of your surroundings.

Almost a Projectile

A tactical flashlight isn't a projectile weapon per se, but if it is bright enough, it does have the power to temporarily blind and disorient an attacker from a distance by simply shining the light directly into his eyes. As a preventive tactic, you can combine this technique with the concepts of boundary setting that we discussed earlier. Since a criminal who has adapted his eyes to darkness is many times more sensitive to light than someone operating in normal lighting conditions, the beam of a high-powered flashlight hits hard. Destroying his night vision and verbally setting boundaries is a powerful combination with a great potential to make him back down. It also gives you a great head start on your escape, since he won't be able to see well enough to follow you effectively.

If that isn't enough, trashing his night vision and immediately following with a low-line kick to the shin or groin is a great alternative, since he literally won't see what hit him. This "flash and smash" tactic is the perfect example of using the beam of the light to act as a "force multiplier." By itself, it's not necessarily a fight stopper; but as a preparatory move for a low-line mobility-kill kick, it's ideal.

Striking with the Flashlight

If for whatever reason the options described above aren't enough, it's time to test the shock resistance of your light. Flashlights make outstanding improvised weapons and can

Used proactively, flashlights remind you to be aware and enable you to scan for and identify potential threats from a distance.

be employed very effectively with the tactics described previously in this book. To make them even more effective, combine them with the use of the light as a blinding tool. Every time you chamber to strike, use the natural tightening of your grip to hit the switch and activate the light. With a little practice, your cycling rhythm can incorporate a blinding shot of light into the attacker's face the moment before you hit—again, an application of the "flash and smash" tactic.

Because a good tactical flashlight provides an excellent grip, you can use it to hit very hard without fear of damaging your hand. That means that you can hit just about anything you want; however, the most effective targets include the face, temples, ears, jaw, collarbones, sternum, and hands.

As mentioned earlier, strikes with an improvised weapon are not guaranteed to take an attacker completely out of the fight. Again, you'll want to back up your flashlight cycling with the same low-line knees and kicks that you use to back up your empty-hand tactics and other improvised-weapon tactics. Strike to create the desired high-line damage and reaction and then finish the fight with the low-line mobility kill. If it sounds like I'm repeating myself, I am. Have a plan, and work your plan.

In case you're wondering if it's necessary to have a crenulated bezel (a scalloped texture on the rim of the bezel, supposedly to focus the impact) on your light, it's not. A plain bezel hits plenty hard and does not raise any eyebrows when going through places like airport security. Although "weaponizing" your light may marginally improve its function as a striking tool, it may also cause you the kind of negative attention that could ultimately deny you the opportunity to carry that tool.

Drills Develop Skills

The best way to develop skills is through repetition. And the best way to achieve high numbers of repetitions is through well-structured drills. The Cycling Drill is a basic, easily learned partner drill that provides an excellent framework to develop your cycling technique. It also introduces the concept of reflex training drills or "flow" drills, which I believe are critical to efficient personal-defense skill development.

To perform the Cycling Drill drill, face your training partner at about an arm's length distance. Both of you should be "armed" with a flashlight or suitable training substitute. Have your partner start the drill by striking at your head with his flashlight with a downward hammer-style blow (the second action of the cycling technique). As his strike approaches,

The "flash and smash" tactic involves using the flashlight to momentarily blind an attacker so you can take the cheap shot and hit him when he's defenseless. Here an attack is countered with a blast of light and kick to the groin.

When wielded with basic gross motor skills, the flashlight also makes a powerful impact weapon.

parry it inward and downward with your left palm, as in the first motion of cycling. As you complete your parry, immediately follow with your right-hand strike to your partner's head. As your strike approaches him, he should parry with his left palm—just as you did—and strike again with his right.

Once you establish a "flow" with this drill, you'll see that each of your right-hand attacks prompts the other's left-hand defense. The result is a true cyclical pattern that allows both of you many repetitions in a short period of time. It also teaches you realistic timing, distance, impact and resistance in the application of your left-hand defensive skills. By varying the speed and intensity of the drill, you can also create enough performance anxiety to simulate the type of stress you will experience in an actual fight.

After you are thoroughly familiar with the basic drill, incorporate the "force multiplier" aspect of the light into your movements. As you chamber for each hammerfist strike, activate the light and shine it directly in your partner's eyes before you strike. In practice, you can avoid actually blinding your partner by using a dimming filter or a simple piece of masking tape over the flashlight bezel.

Obviously, this drill can also be easily adapted to empty-hand training by replacing the flashlight fist load with an open palm or hammerfist. You can also simulate an attacker/defender scenario by arming one partner with a different training weapon, like a training knife or stick. This teaches you do defend against larger, more capable weapons by parrying the weapon-wielding hand and to constantly adjust your distance to put you close enough to strike with your flashlight.

Flashlights and Firearms: Low-Light Tactics

If firearms are part of your personal-defense plan, you also need to consider the use of flashlights in conjunction with your shooting tactics. However, in doing so, I believe it is critically important that you structure your tactics to be appropriate to your actual needs.

Many shooting schools and training courses address low-light tactics. In most cases, they do this from a gun-centric perspective that is more relevant to a law enforcement officer or duty-bound armed professional than a civilian concerned with personal and family defense. While learning to clear rooms with a light and a handgun is fun and can definitely challenge your skills as a shooter, *just because you know how to do something doesn't mean you actually have a need to do it.*

To illustrate this point, let's consider the typical low-light training exercise that is presented at many shooting schools. You're standing outside a shoot house with a holstered

Flashlight Tactics

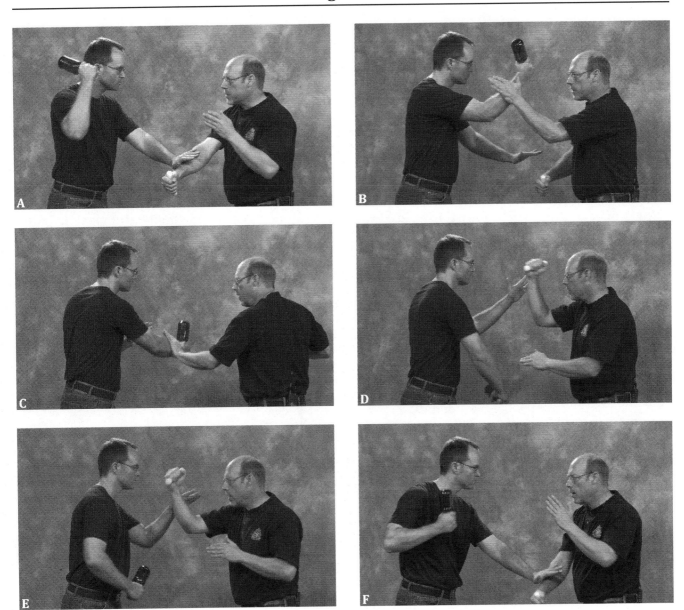

The Cycling Drill is a simple partner training drill that develops timing, reflexes, accuracy, and speed in the application of cycling technique.

gun, extra magazines, and your trusty flashlight. The instructor explains that there are an unknown number of armed people in the house. You must go in and, using your light and gun, identify and neutralize the bad guys without shooting any innocents.

As a shooting exercise, this may sound fun and challenging. However, as a logical solution to that real-world problem—especially for a civilian—it's ridiculous. As a civilian presented with that problem, the best use of your flashlight would be to find your cell phone so you could call 911 and wait for the SWAT team to arrive.

Some might argue that such a scenario actually represents your response to a suspicious noise in the middle of the night. You have to move through your house to your kid's room, secure him or her, and move back to your safe room. While that's more plausible, if you are truly committed to keeping your family safe, the underlying logic of that scenario is still flawed. Instead of spending money to learn tactics that are beyond the scope of reasonable home defense, you might be better served by investing in an alarm system for your house or remodeling to move your child's room closer to yours. Those changes would have a much more profound and immediate effect on your family's security than your house-clearing skills.

With all this in mind, let's consider the logic of using a light in conjunction with a firearm from the ground up. Since we're concerned with both home defense and personal defense in public, let's concentrate primarily on handguns. Most low-light training addresses using a flashlight to compensate for a lack of adequate ambient light to search for, locate, identify, and effectively engage hostile threats. In that context, the major focus is typically on marrying the light-bearing hand and gun-bearing hand to achieve the best possible two-handed shooting position and, in the process, to get the light beam and the bore line to coincide as closely as possible. When this is all considered in the context of the typical square-range scenario (i.e. there's a bad guy or multiple bad guys downrange who are armed with lethal weapons), it all makes sense and seems to support the goal. It also suggests that weapon-mounted lights are a great idea, since they integrate the light and gun into a single, easy-to-grip unit.

However, if we consider the potential of the hand-held flashlight that we've already discussed—as an awareness tool, a non-lethal means of disrupting an attacker's vision, and a carry-anywhere less-lethal impact tool—it's obvious that its defensive application goes far beyond its use in conjunction with a gun. More importantly, if we think about the basic rules of gunhandling and gun safety, it becomes obvious that the default tactic of blindly marrying the light and the gun together is a potential recipe for disaster.

To illustrate this, let's consider one of the most popular flashlight shooting methods: the Harries flashlight technique. A favorite of Weaver-style shooters, it involves crossing the hand holding the light under your gun hand and pressing the backs of your hands together to stabilize the structure and closely align both light and muzzle. In our hypothetical "bump-in-the-middle-of-the-night" scenario, many shooters would be tempted to grab a pistol and a light, assume this position, and start searching the house for the source of the noise. Let's explore the logic of that approach.

One of the four cardinal rules of gun safety is "Never let your muzzle cover anything you're not willing to destroy." That makes great sense and is one of the foundations of responsible gunhandling skills. However, when you think

Flashlight shooting positions that lock the light and the bore line together require you to point the muzzle at everything you illuminate—a potentially dangerous practice.

Flashlight Tactics

of that in the context of the Harries position (or any other hands-together flashlight shooting position), the light and muzzle are always aligned. As such, functionally you are "willing to destroy" anything you shine your light at. If you are searching your house for the source of a suspicious noise, you could easily be shining that light at the dog, your kids raiding the fridge, or sleepwalking grandpa. While the Harries technique is great for getting hits on target in low-light shooting exercises or as a search position for duty-bound officers, for a civilian in the middle of the night in his own home, it means pointing your gun at anything in the dark—including your loved ones.

Using the flashlight independently of the gun allows you to use the light freely while maintaining good muzzle discipline.

Returning to the context of personal defense outside your home, the utility of two-handed shooting methods is even more questionable. Again, let's look at a plausible context: It's late, you are leaving work (or any other safe haven) and you have to walk through an area of darkness to get to your car. On your route, you are suddenly confronted by an unknown person who may or may not be a threat. Because the ambient lighting is inadequate, you can't clearly identify him as a threat, but his attitude, behavior, and mannerisms give you reasonable cause for concern. You are legally armed with a handgun and you also have a hand-held flashlight. In this situation, the less-lethal use of the light must take priority. Your best tactic would be to use the light to illuminate the unknown person and determine whether he is truly a threat or not and, if he is, if he is armed in such a way as to constitute a potentially lethal threat. Until you've established that he's a potentially lethal threat, you aren't legally justified in drawing your gun and all the cool-guy two-handed shooting methods in the world won't do you any good. For this reason, if you opt to carry a firearm with a weapon-mounted light, you also need to carry a hand-held light that you can use independent of your firearm for the vast majority of personal-defense (and non-defense-related) situations that don't justify the introduction of a firearm.

Knowing is the Difference

If you *know* you are facing a potentially lethal threat and might be forced to engage that threat with a handgun, a two-handed shooting position or weapon-mounted light makes perfect sense. The key word here is *knowing* that you're facing that threat.

For example, a SWAT team performing a tactical entry *knows* that it's going in harm's way. For all intents and purposes, they are also acting offensively. While they must certainly exercise extreme judgment to avoid endangering innocent parties, they're basically operating on their terms.

Conversely, a civilian—particularly a CCW holder out in public—faces a very different set of circumstances. In that context, you will almost always be *reacting* to the circumstances around you and must do so in ways that are appropriate to those circumstances. Since you are not duty bound to become involved in an incident, you are free to avoid potentially dangerous situations and should seek safe escape. You also cannot draw or brandish a firearm without serious justification.

With all that in mind, let's put things back into a personal-defense context. Confronted by a potential threat, you have your light in hand and are doing everything right. You are trying to maintain distance by using verbal skills and physical posturing. The light is in your power hand ready for a "flash and smash" or to be used as an impact weapon. As you do all this, you are watching the person in front of you intently, paying close attention to his hands. Suddenly, he starts to lift his shirt and reach for something in his waistband.

Based on your belief that he is armed and the fact that you are now in fear for your life, it's now time to bring your gun into play. Ideally, you want to retain the ability to use your light, so you must pass it from your right hand to your left to be able to draw. The easiest way to do this is to bring your hands together in front of you and "roll" it from your right hand into your left hand. This movement is very easily learned and keeps the light under control the entire time.

Once it is transferred to the left hand, the light is gripped in the same "fist" grip as it was in the right with the bezel on the little-finger side of the hand. Bring your left hand up to your temple as a guard as your right hand clears your cover garment, achieves a proper grip, and draws the gun to a weapon-retention position. From that position, you can either fire one handed if the assailant closes with you or extend your arm to shoot from a more conventional one-hand position. Either way, the light stays where it is—as part of a solid guard that protects your head and keeps your left hand well away from the muzzle.

Why not just carry the light in your left/non-firearm hand from the very start? Again, that only makes sense if you *know* that you're going to face a potentially lethal threat and will have to draw your gun. If you don't know that, holding it in your weak hand limits your ability to use it as an impact weapon.

If transitioning the light from one hand to the other seems too complicated to perform under stress, remember that you are free to do so at any time if you feel justified. If you are facing someone who is behaving suspiciously and won't show you his hands, transition the light and prep your draw. That action may convince him to back down. Alternately, if things unfold quickly and you can't pass the light to your support hand, throw it at him and then draw. If you can get him to duck and cover for even an instant, you increase your chances of getting your gun into play.

Full-Spectrum Versatility

The flashlight is an incredibly versatile tool and, in my opinion, one of the most important elements of a sound personal defense kit. For people who are uncomfortable with the idea of carrying a purpose-designed weapon like a knife or firearm, it is also a great "entry-level" tool to get used to the idea of carrying some type of self-defense implement. It is an excellent reminder to be aware and alert, it allows you to illuminate your environment to look for possible threats, it can be used to blind an assailant to give you a momentary advantage to preemptively disable him, it can be used as an impact weapon, and, yes, it can also be a headlight for your handgun. But, just as the gun itself does not represent a full-service self-defense strategy, the light—viewed only as an accompaniment to the gun—doesn't either.

See the light—and the logic to use it to its fullest potential.

CHAPTER 8: DEFENSIVE USE OF THE CANE

Choosing a weapon for personal defense is a balancing act. While you definitely want the most potent weapon possible, you also need to ensure that you have something appropriate for non-lethal threats that don't justify the use of lethal force. At the same time, you must ensure that the weapon you choose can be conveniently carried on a daily basis and that it is legally permissible wherever you live or travel.

If you ponder those requirements for a while, you'll quickly realize that traditional weapon choices like handguns, knives, purpose-designed impact weapons and even pepper spray don't meet all the criteria—especially if you factor in non-permissive environments and situations like air travel. One of the few weapons that does qualify is the humble cane or walking stick.

Throughout history, the cane has been a fashion accessory and personal-defense weapon in many cultures; however, in modern times, it is primarily regarded as a mobility aid for people with physical disabilities or injuries. This image of the cane, along with the fact that no medical justification is required to use one, qualify it as the ultimate "PC" weapon—but only if it is powered by a functional skill set.

Before we examine the details of what constitutes practical cane technique, let's accept the fact that we all get old. As such, we need to understand the difference between being an able-bodied person who *chooses* to carry a cane and being an older person who may *need* to carry one. Obviously, the more limited your physical attributes, the simpler and more effective your tactics need to be.

We also need to draw a hard line between "martial arts" and actual "self-defense." Self-defense is simple: It is all about stopping your attacker from hurting you by either disabling him or causing enough direct, unavoidable pain that he chooses to quit and victimize someone else. Conversely, holding him in a complicated martial-artsy joint lock while you hope he finds religion is not a direct route to personal safety.

With all that in mind, the unfortunate truth is that most cane "systems" being taught today are far too complicated and too physically intense to qualify as practical self-defense—especially for someone who relies on a cane as a mobility aid. Faced with that truth, I set out to develop a cane system that could be learned with a minimum of training time, be simple enough to remember and retain without much regular practice, and, most importantly, be physically achievable by people with limited physical attributes. Building on these requirements, I also wanted the system to be versatile enough so that folks who do have the benefit of greater strength can pursue a higher skill set if they choose to. As they age, if their physical abilities diminish, they can "scale" their tactics accordingly. That system is known as Martial Cane Concepts (MCC).

MCC is based on the idea of using simple, easily learned sequences of movement as the basis for a wide variety of combative applications. Like the empty-hand tactics and improvised-weapon tactics addressed in previous chapters, the idea with a cane is to "have a plan, and work your plan." By understanding that all motions have multiple potential applications, you can learn, apply, and adapt techniques to real defensive situations very quickly.

The Guard

The basic MCC combination begins from the guard position, which is adapted from the Filipino stick fighting art of De Cuerdas Eskrima. If you are right handed, place your left foot forward so your feet are about shoulder width apart and slightly staggered. Grip the shaft of the cane near the handle with your right hand in a natural "fist" grip and raise the tip of the cane in front of your body. With your left hand, grasp the shaft of the cane about one-third up from the tip with a palm-down grip, keeping your thumb and all four fingers on top of the cane shaft. Draw your right elbow in close to your body so your right hand is near your hip and center the tip of the cane in front of your face at eye level. In this guard, the cane functions as a shield against incoming attacks and is perfectly positioned for effective striking. It is also close to your body so you can retain control of it easily and employ it effectively in confined spaces.

The Basic MCC Sequence

The core of the MCC system is a basic sequence of six movements. From the guard position, this sequence is performed as follows:

- Drop your weight slightly and execute a sharp, two-handed downward motion with the tip of the cane, lowering it to about solar plexus height.
- Thrust forward at a slightly upward angle, driving with the power of both arms. A slight shuffle step forward will increase the power of this thrust.
- Loosen the grip of your left hand and slide it toward your right as you point the cane straight up. Place your left hand on the thumb side of your right wrist for support. This allows you to grip the cane with one hand, yet swing it with the power of both.
- Execute a fast forehand swing (like swinging

The Martial Cane Concepts guard positions the cane in front of the body where it serves as both a shield and a striking weapon.

Defensive Use of the Cane

a baseball bat) targeting the attacker's knees or shins and follow through to your left side, letting the cane wrap around you and stop at your left shoulder.
- Execute a fast backhand swing, again targeting the attacker's knees or shins. Follow through to your right side, turning your right hand palm up and allowing the cane to stop at your right shoulder.
- Lower the tip of the cane and return to the guard position.

Practice this sequence slowly and build it step by step. As you get more familiar with it, gradually increase the speed and power of your strikes and swings. In the process, you'll learn a lot about your cane and your ability to wield it effectively. If you find that it's too heavy, too

The basic Martial Cane Concepts sequence is designed to provide many defensive applications in a single, easy-to-learn package that is practical for people who actually need canes for mobility.

light, or doesn't offer a secure grip, shop around for a better one that has the attributes you need to make your tactics work.

Defensive Applications

Once you feel comfortable with the basic MCC sequence, it's time to explore how it can be applied defensively against common types of attacks. One very likely possibility is that when you assume your guard position, your attacker will grab the tip of your cane. Against this attack, the abrupt downward snap of the first motion of the sequence uses the strength of both arms and your body weight to break that grip. This action will also pull your attacker forward into the second movement: the two-handed thrust, which has great effect when targeted at the solar plexus, sternum, throat, or face. It will also typically send your attacker reeling backward and create an opportunity for the finishing blow: that full-power swing to the knee, shin, or ankle—or what I call a "mobility kill."

Mobility kills are central to the MCC system for two reasons: First, by damaging the legs, you destroy the attacker's ability to stand and fight, as well as his ability to pursue you when you escape. This is particularly important if you actually must use a cane for mobility and cannot escape quickly.

The lower legs are also a preferred target because they are very easy for you to hit and exceedingly difficult for your attacker to protect. High strikes—to the head or neck—are easily blocked; but strikes to the legs take best advantage of the length and power of the cane and are very difficult to stop.

My favorite target for this tactic is the attacker's shin. It is larger, easier to hit, and harder to defend than the knee, and when struck with full power is excruciatingly painful. If for whatever reason your first strike to the knee or shin is not successful or if you miss, you'll find that the basic sequence already provides the back-up tactic you need. Just follow through on your strike, chamber on the left side of your body, and swing for the shins again. That portion of the sequence—alternating low strikes to the legs—can be isolated and repeated as necessary and is an excellent way of creating distance and dealing with multiple attackers.

Punch Defense

One technique often taught in traditional cane systems is to parry an incoming punch by whipping the tip end of the cane upward with a snap of the wrist. This requires great speed, wrist strength, and timing—all things that a real cane user may not possess.

Even if you did have the strength and skill to move your cane with exceptional speed, this technique is still extremely impractical. Do the math: Your attacker's fist is traveling straight at your head from two feet away. You have to rotate the tip of a three-foot stick from the ground up in a 180-degree arc and deflect the punch before it hits you. It doesn't make sense.

Instead, use the standard sequence. The initial downward motion can be used to strike the fist or forearm of the incoming hand or, even better, the two-handed thrust can be used as a "stop-hit" to the attacker's shoulder or chest.

Many traditional cane systems teach blocking and deflecting punches with the shaft of the cane. Even if you are highly skilled, it offers a poor chance of success.

Defensive Use of the Cane

Skip the initial motion altogether and just thrust into the chest to stop the punch cold. This also illustrates the fact that you don't have to use all the movements of the sequence; feel free to start late or end early as the situation requires.

Remember also that just because you have a cane doesn't mean that your empty-hand tactics won't work. Since your hand moves faster and more naturally that the cane, parry the punch with your left hand and raise the cane straight up into the attacker's groin. Functionally, those movements are identical to raising the cane into the basic guard position, so they still qualify as part of the basic sequence.

Chokes and Grabs

If an attacker manages to grab you or choke you, you know exactly where his hands are and you know for a fact that they are "busy." Step back into your guard position and proceed directly to the two-handed thrust to the sternum or throat to drive him back and break his grip. Once his grip is broken, complete the sequence and break his shinbones as well.

Weapon Defense

What if the attack is a strike with a weapon like a tire iron? In this case, use the cane as a shield by pivoting in the direction of the strike and opening your left hand as you snap the shaft forward to block the weapon. Opening your hand so only the palm contacts the cane protects your fingers while still blocking with the power of both arms.

Once the attacker's weapon has been stopped, turn back to center and slide your cane down the length of his weapon to smash his fingers, potentially disarming him. Then, simply complete the rest of the sequence to end the encounter.

If all this sounds too simple, we're on the right track, because self-defense should be simple. The cane is an incredibly potent weapon and one of the few personal-defense tools capable of "flying below the radar" virtually anywhere you go. Power it with a practical system of tactics that you can count on for the rest of your life and you'll never walk alone again.

A better tactic is to use the thrusting action of the basic sequence and the length of the cane for a "shoulder stop." This short-circuits the punch before it can land and hits with devastating impact.

Here the basic MCC sequence is used to defeat a stick attack. First, pivot into the strike, open your left hand to protect your fingers, and block using the shaft of the cane supported by both hands. Then, pivot back to center and perform the basic MCC sequence, striking down on the attacker's hand, thrusting into his head, neck, or chest, and finishing with a powerful "mobility kill" strike to the shin.

CHAPTER 9: PEPPER SPRAY BASICS

In a self-defense situation, size does matter. In simple terms, the less physically capable you are, the less able you are to defend yourself against a violent attack—especially if your attacker is significantly larger and stronger than you are.

One of the most effective ways of "evening the odds" is to target an attacker's vision. Even the toughest guy can't strengthen his eyes, and if he can't see you, he can't attack you effectively.

Based on this premise, pepper spray (also known as "OC" or oleoresin capsicum) is an extremely practical and effective personal defense weapon. It not only directly affects an attacker's vision; it allows you to do it from a safe distance.

OC is a chemical compound that irritates the eyes to cause tears, pain, and even temporary blindness. It also affects breathing, causing debilitating coughing and choking. It was developed by Professor James H. Jenkins and Dr. Frank Hayes, D.V.M. at the University of Georgia in 1960 and first sold in 1963 under the brand name "Halt Animal Repellant." Initially intended as a defense against vicious animals, it later attracted the attention of the Federal Bureau of Investigation, which saw it as a potential alternative to physical confrontation or the use of lethal force. In 1989, after three years of extensive testing by their Firearms Training Unit (FTU), the FBI authorized OC for use by its special agents and SWAT teams. Other law enforcement agencies followed suit and by the early 1990's it was in widespread use by more than 3,000 agencies in the U.S.

By the late 1990's, pepper spray also became popular in the civilian sector. Affordable, effective, and non-lethal, it is also extremely convenient and legal to own and carry in most jurisdictions. These qualities make it as near-perfect personal-defense tool and have driven the development of a wide variety of pepper spray products targeted at the civilian market. However, like any other tool, the most effective application of OC requires proper tactics and a proper understanding of its limitations.

How Hot is Hot?

The active ingredient in pepper spray is capsaicin, a chemical derived from the fruit of plants in the genus Capsicum, which includes chili peppers. It is extracted by grinding the peppers into a fine powder and mixing it with an organic solvent like ethanol. When the ethanol is evaporated, the remaining resin is the oleoresin capsicum. This process and the peppers used in it determine the "hotness" of the base resin, which is measured in Scoville Heat Units (SHU). However, this alone does not determine how hot the spray is.

To deliver the capsaicin in the resin as an aerosol, it is mixed with an emulsifier that allows it to be suspended in water. Some sprays also contain an ultraviolet marking dye that can help in identifying an attacker if he is apprehended by the police. The potency of the final mixture is therefore a combination of the hotness of the base resin and the percentage of resin in the final solution. As such, although some manufacturers tout a high percentage of OC in their spray, it doesn't necessarily reflect a more potent product. To ensure that your spray is effective, choose a reputable brand with a proven track record, preferably based on use by law enforcement agencies.

Choosing an OC Spray

OC comes in a wide variety of formats, ranging from ultra compact sprays that attach to a keychain to super-sized home-defense units. Like any personal-protection weapon, if you hope to have it when you need it, you must make the commitment to carry it consistently. Convenience of carry is therefore a major consideration.

The smallest OC sprays are roughly the size of your thumb and can therefore be conveniently carried in a pocket or on a keychain. Some are also made to look like pens and can be carried just as easily. While these features make them easy to carry consistently, it can also make them difficult to use under stress when fine motor skills degrade. Small sprays also have limited capacity and some only offer a few brief bursts and limited range.

Slightly larger sprays (around 15-22 grams in size) often feature plastic or metal clips that allow them to be attached to the top of a pocket or the inside of a purse. Although they are larger and require more commitment to carry, they are easier to grasp and operate under stress and can deliver more shots than their smaller counterparts—an important consideration if you face multiple attackers. Larger sprays can also serve as impact weapons if the spray itself doesn't do the job. For serious personal protection, these sprays are typically your best choice.

Two other key aspects of choosing an OC spray are its spray pattern and the consistency

Pepper sprays come in many shapes and sizes. Do your homework and choose a format that you will carry consistently and can bring into action quickly.

of the solution. Spray patterns for liquid OC typically include cones and streams. A cone, also often called a fog, is a fine mist that has a broad pattern and lingers in the air. It requires less accuracy when sprayed and can be used in an "area denial" mode; however, it has a shorter effective range and is easily affected by wind. Streams are just as the name implies—focused, narrow jets of spray. They have a longer range and are less affected by wind, but require greater accuracy to achieve the desired effect. Many street criminals have also learned how to shield themselves against streams by covering their faces with their arms, hats, or clothing.

Other types of pepper sprays include foams and gels. Like streams, these have a long effective range, but also offer a thicker viscosity that sticks to the attacker. Again, these sprays require accuracy, but buck the wind fairly well.

One final consideration is the type if trigger. Most smaller sprays are thumb operated, which is consistent with the gross motor skills that take over under stress. They also allow you to use your thumb as a guide for accuracy and to extend the spray away from your body. Kubotan-style OC sprays also have thumb triggers, but fire from the bottom—requiring a bent-arm position that puts the spray closer to your own face when firing.

Choose Your Battlefield—And Your Spray

With these factors in mind, your first "tactic" should be to choose a type of spray that is appropriate to the conditions where you are most likely to use it. If your biggest fear is being attacked in an enclosed area, a fog that forces you to share the effects of the spray with your attacker is not your best choice. Wide open, but consistently windy places are also not conducive to the use of fogs. They either won't reach your attacker or, even worse, may blow back on you. Conversely, if your biggest fear is being attacked in a covered parking garage that is blocked from the wind, a fog could be an excellent choice.

Once you choose a spray, it is also very important that you test fire it so you can see firsthand what kind of pattern it creates and how far it reaches. Good OC manufacturers often offer inert training versions of their sprays that are ideal for practicing your skills. If you can't find these, buy two of your preferred spray and use one for testing and the other to carry.

Carry Concepts

If you want to rely on a weapon for self-defense, you must carry it religiously and do so in a way that keeps it instantly accessible. Pepper sprays come in a wide variety of shapes, sizes, and configurations. That's both a good and a bad thing, since some seemingly convenient spray formats can be extremely difficult to

Stream, gel, and foam-style pepper sprays typically have a greater range than fogs and are less likely to blow back on you; however, they require greater accuracy.

employ under the stress of an actual attack. For example, some pepper sprays are available in a format that looks like a pen. While this style of spray can be easily clipped to a shirt pocket for quick access, removing the cap requires two hands and orienting the spray direction isn't easily accomplished by feel alone. As such, it's not a practical draw-and-spray weapon; it needs to be in your hand and ready to go before it's needed.

Small sprays also tend to have limited payloads. If you're concerned about multiple attackers (you should be), a spray with multiple-shot capability is a must.

As with any other weapon, the rule when carrying pepper spray is to carry it the same way all the time. That way, when you need it, you know exactly where is and the skills you've developed o draw it will take you there. To support this goal, take a look at the way you dress and the type of spray you want to carry and determine how they can fit together. For example, if you typically wear jeans or other pants with a watch pocket adjacent to the right front pocket, it is an excellent home for a small can of OC. A 22-gram (just under one ounce), multi-shot can fits perfectly in that pocket and keeps your spray accessible for immediate use.

Although keychain-style OC sprays would seem to be a great solution to convenient carry, they don't necessarily offer immediate access. The time it takes for you dig in your pocket, extract your keys, fumble for the spray, orient it, and remove the safety is time you'll never have when responding to a sudden attack. Keychain-mounted OC jumbled in the bottom of a purse is even worse.

In simple terms, if you want to have a prayer of drawing and using your OC in response to a spontaneous incident, you need to carry it in such a way that you can access, draw, orient, and prep it to fire with only one hand in three seconds or less. To do that, you need to be intimately familiar with the operation of your spray and be able to draw and operate it based on tactile sense (feel) alone. That means practicing your draw regularly and making it second nature.

The Best Draw is No Draw

If mastering an OC quick draw sounds like work, it is. If you're not willing to invest that effort—or if carrying OC in support of a quick draw doesn't work for you—your best tactic is to have it in hand whenever you think you might need it. For this tactic, keychain-style OC sprays work well because the keys hide your intent. Walking around with your keys in your hand is perfectly normal. Walking around with a can of

Test firing pepper spray is an important step in understanding the pattern and range of your spray. Ideally, get an inert training spray. If one is not available, buy two live units and use one for testing. Here the author tests a fog-style home defense spray from Sabre Red.

Pepper Spray Basics

OC gets people spun up.

Although this may sound easy, it takes practice. Before you leave any safe haven—your office, your house, etc.—you need to stop and put your OC in your hand before you walk out the door. The act of moving the spray from pocket or purse to hand must become fluid and automatic. Once in your hand, hold your spray so you can instantly disarm the safety and use the spray if necessary. With practice, you'll achieve a comfortable but always-armed demeanor.

Use Your Words

Getting your OC in your hand is half the battle. The other half is using it defensively. The best way to do that is to integrate it into the verbal and physical skills you've already learned from this book.

For example, let's say you have your OC in your right, dominant hand and are approached by a suspicious person. Before he gets to close, raise your left hand, palm forward and tell him to "Stay back." As you do this, keep your right hand and the spray close to your body, but oriented in his direction. These actions combine the ready position we discussed in the sections on unarmed tactics and improvised weapons with our verbal and boundary-setting skills.

If the situation escalates and you are unable to dissuade him verbally, the OC allows you to engage him before he gets to close. To do that, first ensure that you deactivate the safety on the spray. Retract your left hand and drive your right hand and the spray straight forward, like throwing a punch. I prefer sprays with top-mounted buttons that can be held in the fist and fired with the thumb. This is consistent with the gross motor skills that dominate during stressful events and much more secure than using the index finger and spraying like paint. The thumb-on-top grip also allows you to instinctively aim the spray by pointing your thumb at the target.

If you have fog-style spray, aim at your attacker's face and move the can in an "S" pattern to create a "wall" of OC mist between you. Don't be stingy, but don't dump the entire can—especially if you're not close enough to ensure that it affects him. Continue to use strong verbal skills as you back up to create distance and look for an escape route. Be prepared to follow up immediately with another shot if he advances.

If you have a stream, gel, or foam-style spray, aim at your attacker's face and paint him from ear to ear. Some street-smart attackers have learned to use their hats and jackets to shield against OC spray. Don't waste your spray on his clothing and pick your shots. Even with his face

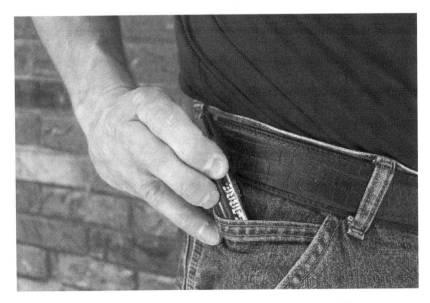

Plan your pepper spray carry to fit your style of dress and practice your draw consistently to ensure that you can get it into action when you need it.

The Best Defense

The ready stance with pepper spray is the same as that used for empty-hand self-defense and the use of improvised weapons—a natural hands-up posture with the power side back. If you need to use the spray, step forward or back to reverse your stance before you spray. This helps you aim accurately and keeps you from spraying your non-weapon hand.

covered, spraying his upper chest can splatter upwards and get enough spray near his face to do the job.

No Guarantees

Pepper spray is not a 100% solution. It is entirely possible that your attacker will continue his assault even after he's been sprayed. If he does, you must have back-up tactics. If you carry another weapon, transition to it. If you don't, apply the simple low-line kicks we discussed earlier to target your attacker's knees, shins, and groin. Hopefully the spray diminished his vision so he won't see them coming. Kick hard to destroy his mobility and create an opportunity for escape.

Some OC sprays are incorporated into Kubotan-style impact weapons that provide a built-in back-up to the spray. While these can definitely be useful, they also require that you get closer to your attacker and the OC you just hosed him with. Obviously, you don't want to share the effects of that OC, so try not to grapple with him. Hit with the Kubotan to create an opportunity for the low-line mobility-killing kick.

Pepper spray can be an incredibly effective personal-defense tool, but only if it is employed with good tactics. Choose it wisely, train with it diligently, and back it up with other sound combative skills.

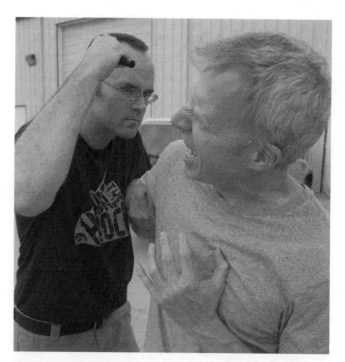

Like any weapon, pepper spray is not guaranteed to work every time. You must therefore be prepared to follow up with other tactics. Kubotan-style sprays are designed to double as impact weapons, but low-line kicks work well also.

CHAPTER 10: KNIVES AND SELF-DEFENSE

When applied with proper tactics, the knife can be an extremely effective personal-defense weapon. Unlike a firearm, it is also legal to carry in some form in every state in the Union and in many foreign countries. As such, it makes the ideal back-up weapon to a handgun and the perfect alternative weapon if you live or travel in areas where the carry of defensive firearms is prohibited.

Unfortunately, there is a lot of misinformation out there when it comes to the use of knives in self-defense. Before you choose to carry a knife as a defensive weapon, your first order of business should be to establish a system of sound logic to guide your efforts and your training. My system of knife tactics, Martial Blade Concepts (MBC), is based on the following logical elements:

- **Accept the fact that you will fight with the knife (or knives) you actually have with you when the attack happens.** Many knife "experts" have pontificated on the requirements of the ideal fighting knife, waxing eloquent about blade lengths, crossguards, handle materials, etc, etc. That's great, but unfortunately the fighting knives they typically recommend cannot be legally or practically carried by the average civilian on a daily basis. Let's face it, the best fighting knife in the world is the one you actually have with you when the fight starts, not the one back home in your sock drawer. Understand this, accept it, and choose your weapon and your training accordingly.

  Research the laws in your area and the areas you typically travel and choose a high-quality knife that is both legal in those jurisdictions and a very potent defensive weapon. If possible, choose a knife that also has a training version that is mechanically identical to your live blade, but allows safe contact training with a partner.

  Then, tune your training to focus on the deployment and practical application of that weapon and make its carry part of your daily lifestyle.

- **Understand and validate the destructive power of your actual carry knife.** Once you have decided what knife you will carry, you need to have a clear understanding of what you can do with it. And the only way to do that is to actually cut and puncture things with it.

By "things," what I really mean are reasonable facsimiles of flesh-and-bone body parts, covered with a realistic layer of clothing. My traditional testing target is a "pork man." No, he is not one of the lesser-known superheroes, but a realistic cutting target made from a pork roast. To construct one, take a five-pound pork roast, butterfly it (cut it lengthwise about halfway through its thickness) and tie it around a one-inch dowel with butcher twine. Then wrap the entire thing in about a half a roll of kitchen plastic wrap, tape down the ends, and cover it with the leg of a pair of jeans. The resulting target is typically a very good facsimile of the average man's forearm, bicep/triceps, or lower thigh.

Needless to say, before you attempt any live-blade cutting tests, you need to have a degree of skill with your knife. You must also go slowly and take extreme care to avoid injury. I recommend working with an unsharpened training knife first and progressing to the live blade only when you're sure you're ready.

When you do progress to the live-blade tests, start out easy and let the blade do the cutting. Don't be in a hurry and take the time to really assess the results of each cut. After you've done a few light cuts, add more body mechanics to the motion and see the difference in the effects on the target. Then, do the same thing with thrusting. The goal is to develop an understanding of the force you're applying and results you're getting on the target so you can relate that to a human attacker.

As you gain more experience and confidence, replace the layer of denim with other types of clothing that are consistent with the seasons and climate where you live. This will help you further realize what your knife can and can't do and what type of protection—if any—different materials offer (that's also useful information when choosing your wardrobe).

- **Accept the fact that stopping power is the ultimate goal of all self-defense.** Any serious student of defensive shooting should be familiar with the term "stopping power." In simple terms, the real goal of all self-defense is to stop your attacker so he is physically incapable of continuing his attack. While some tactics—including the simple act of drawing a weapon with confidence—may be enough to make him unwilling to attack, the basis for true stopping power is physical incapacitation.

  If we accept this goal as valid when it comes to the use of firearms, logically it should also be the basis for all other self-defense tactics. No matter what weapon you use, your objective should be to apply it in such a way that it causes tangible physiological damage to your attacker that, based on sound principles of medical science, will lead to rapid, predictable incapacitation.

  As logical as that may sound, when it comes to the defensive (or, in a broader sense, combative) use of knives, much of what is commonly taught today is misguided and impractical.

- **Study human anatomy and learn what targets you can cut to reliably stop an attacker.** This is perhaps the most difficult aspect of understanding knife tactics because—to put it bluntly—the topic is clouded with misinformation, hype, and bullshit. Rather than going to martial artists, Internet forums, or even military close-combat materials (like the widely touted but wildly inaccurate W.E. Fairbairn "Timetable of Death"), pick up a copy of *Gray's Anatomy* and start talking to ER doctors, paramedics, physical therapists, and actual *medical* professionals who see the results of knife wounds and ask them what stops people and what doesn't.

As you develop an understanding of anatomy and the vulnerabilities of various body parts, relate that knowledge back to your cutting tests. Study the cross-sectional diagrams of body parts in anatomy reference books and correlate those to the depths of the cuts and punctures you achieved on your practice target. To get an idea of *actual* target depths, measure the corresponding part on your body and use a photocopier to enlarge the diagram in the book to full scale. Better yet, do this same thing on one of your well-fed friends (the big kind that you would really fear if he attacked you) and look at how body size affects target depth. To put it bluntly, a thrust to the abdomen with a 3-inch blade will do different damage to a 140-pound marathon runner with six-pack abs than it will to a 300-pound biker with a beer belly. By combining your empirical cutting tests with analysis of target depths on various body sizes, you will get an idea of what targets your knife can *realistically* reach in a fight. This knowledge should have a significant bearing on the knife tactics you choose.

In the process of researching anatomy and the effects of knife wounds, you should also realize and accept the fact that killing and stopping are NOT the same thing. If you inflict a mortal wound on your attacker, but it takes him several minutes to expire, he has plenty of time (not to mention motivation) to continue his attack on you. Conversely, targeting key muscles and connective tissues can immediately disable an attacker and keep you safer than focusing on traditional "lethal" targets.

- **Base your tactics on natural, easily learned movements that take into account human instincts and the natural effects of life-threatening stress.** Good knife tactics should be consistent with your natural reactions to life-threatening stress. In simple terms, the stress of a real attack will provoke a startle response (you crouch, your hands come up, your head tries to turtle into your body, and you typically square off with whatever is trying to kill you) and cause gross motor skills to override fine and complex motor skills. In even simpler terms, think caveman instead of ballet dancer.

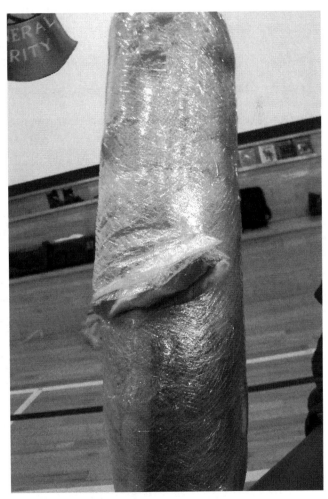

Understanding and quantifying the destructive power of your actual carry knife is an important part of developing realistic knife tactics. "Pork man" is a testing target that consists of a pork roast tied around a wooden dowel. Wrapped with multiple layers of plastic to replicate skin, the resulting target is an analog for human arms and legs—the most effective disabling targets.

Although it is possible to train to overcome—or at least mitigate—instinctive reactions to stress so you can apply complicated tactics, this takes lots of time and very intense training that replicates the stress of real attacks. The average person (and most intelligent above-average people) will instead accept the fact that they will respond instinctively and build their tactics on the foundation of that instinct.

In the realm of knife tactics, this means that simple, straightforward tactics that rely on gross motor movements are your best bet. If you can't grasp the basic mechanics of a technique within a few tries, it's probably not something that's going to work well for you under stress. Also, you need to bear in mind that simple things are easier to remember and easier to program as reflex. If you're not going to train regularly, but still want to have some basic knife tactics in your arsenal, keep them simple.

My MBC program is based on the fundamental principles and proven tactics of the Filipino arts—arguably some of the most effective edged-weapon systems ever devised. Using those tactics as a foundation, I adapted them to focus on the concept of stopping power to make them adaptable to the modern self-defense in the legal climate of Western society.

MBC and is centered on the concept of *Cinco Teros* – the five cardinal blows. Rather than the 12 angles taught in most traditional Filipino systems, I limit the number to five and relate these angles directly to a system of four zones, much like the quadrants of fencing. An angle 1 strike would target an opponent's Zone 1 – the upper left portion of his body. Angle 2 attacks Zone 2 – the upper right. Angle 3 focuses on Zone 3 – the lower left, and Angle 4 targets Zone 4 – the lower right. Angle 5 is a straight thrust along the centerline and may be delivered high or low.

MBC's zone concept allows the student to easily identify any strike based its intended target. For example, any attack that enters Zone 1 is treated as an angle 1. This applies regardless of the type of weapon, the opponent's grip on the weapon, and whether the weapon is held with the left or right hand.

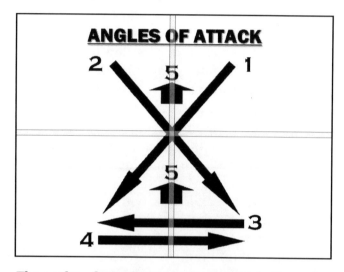

The angles of attack are a template for knife cutting and thrusting tactics. More importantly, they define the "receiving point of view," dividing the defender's space into four quadrants and the centerline.

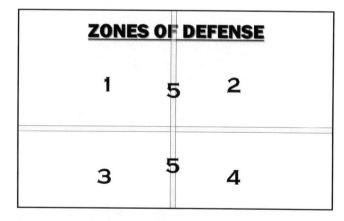

The Zones of Defense represent the "receiving point of view" of the angles of attack. All attacks toward you are viewed through this template, allowing you to instantly identify and categorize them based on the zones of your body they target. For example, all attacks to the upper left quadrant of your body target Zone 1, therefore they are categorized as angle 1 attacks.

Once an attack has been identified as a particular angle, the MBC practitioner has only four basic methods of dealing with that attack. These are called "Defensive Responses." The first is a "pass," which is performed by evading the strike with footwork and body angling and simultaneously cutting the opponent's weapon-wielding wrist or forearm. A "follow" also relies on evading the strike, but the counter is delivered after the opponent's hand crosses your centerline and follows the same direction of movement of his strike. A "meet" is a direct cut to the wrist or forearm of the weapon arm, immediately followed by a block or check with the back of the forearm of the "live" (non-weapon-wielding) hand. This tactic is used when the practitioner cannot or chooses not to evade an opponent's strike. Finally, a *crossada* is a pass that is amplified by slapping or pushing the attacker's weapon hand into the force of the knife's cut. This motion greatly increases the power of the cut and the opponent's vulnerability to a follow-up strike.

Based on this system of four Defensive Zones and four Defensive Responses per zone, the core of the MBC system consists of 16 easily learned techniques. This keeps the practitioner's "decision loop" short and helps promote quick reflexes. Against Angle 5 attacks—straight thrusts along the centerline—the practitioner is taught to use his live hand to redirect the thrust across his centerline and into one of the four zones. At that point, he is in the same physical relationship to his attacker's limb as he would be if he were defending against one of the four primary angles and simply uses an appropriate technique for that angle.

Note that all the Defensive Responses in the MBC system target the attacker's weapon-bearing hand. This is consistent with the Filipino concept of "defanging the snake" and attacking the attacking limb. However, in MBC, I take that concept further and focus on "structural stopping power." This is in direct contrast to the tactics of most traditional knife systems, which focus on the lethality of the knife to achieve stopping power. This approach—especially when applied with small, legal-to-carry knives—is fundamentally flawed.

W.E. Fairbairn's "Timetable of Death"

One of the most common misconceptions about defensive knife tactics has to do with blood loss ("exsanguination," to use the technical term) and its relationship to stopping an attacker. While it is very true that inflicting severe bleeding wounds can ultimately take an attacker out of the fight, it takes much longer for someone to bleed to unconsciousness than most people think. And the longer an armed attacker is upright, mobile, and dangerous, the greater your chances of suffering a serious or potentially mortal wound.

Much of the misinformation regarding blood loss in knife fighting can be traced back to the classic "Timetable of Death" published by British close-combat legend W.E. Fairbairn. Originally featured in the 1942 book *All-In Fighting* and later in the 1944 classic *Get Tough*, the timetable is a diagram of the human body identifying the major arteries and a companion table. The table details the depths below the skin of the various arterial targets and the heart and lists in specific detail exactly how long it takes for a person to bleed to unconsciousness and bleed to death when each of these targets is severed or punctured.

Fairbairn's methodology for developing the timetable has long been the subject of speculation, yet many self-defense practitioners still consider it gospel because it came from such a revered source. One person who did question it was the late Christopher Grosz, a former law enforcement officer and defensive tactics instructor in Littleton, Colorado.

Grosz did extensive independent research into the medical effects of edged weapon wounds and consulted recognized medical experts, including Colorado's Arapahoe County Medical Examiner Dr. Michael Doberson. Based on this research, Grosz developed a simple, scientifically sound method to calculate time to unconsciousness and death based on blood loss. In the process, he also determined that Fairbairn's timetable was extremely inaccurate. For example, according to Fairbairn, a severed carotid artery would cause unconsciousness in 5 seconds and death in 12. Based on Grosz' formula, even at a maximum heart rate of 220 beats per minute unconsciousness will occur after 68 seconds and death after 91 seconds. Clearly, relying on blood loss—even that caused by a severed carotid artery—is not an efficient means of stopping an attacker. Although he may in fact die from his wound, he will have ample opportunity to try to kill you before he does.

Structural Stopping Power

Blood loss stops an attacker (eventually) by stopping his entire body. To achieve quicker incapacitation, it makes more sense to disable the body parts of your attacker that allow him to be dangerous to you. And the best way to do that is by destroying the motor functions that power them.

If you want to consciously move a part of your body, your brain transmits messages to the appropriate muscles. The muscles contract and pull on tendons, which are anchored to the muscle at one end and to a bone at the other end. In simple terms, movement is achieved when muscles pull on tendons to move bones. Logically, if the muscle or tendons are severed, the physical connection of those parts is destroyed and the motor function they produce stops instantly.

Again, the prime example of this in edged-weapon tactics is what the Filipino martial arts refer to as "defanging the snake." When someone attacks with a hand-held weapon, he extends his arm toward you to strike. In doing so, he typically presents the inside of his wrist and forearm, which contain the muscles and flexor tendons that enable him to close his fingers to grip his weapon. Cutting the muscles on the inside of the forearm or the tendons on the inside of the wrist can instantly destroy the structure that supports his grip. If this tactic is executed properly, his hand (the "snake") will involuntarily open and he will drop his weapon (the "fang").

In the event that your initial cut doesn't result in a disarm, the best course of action is to continue to apply the concept of selective incapacitation by targeting other muscle groups that provide critical functions. These include the bicep and triceps muscles of the upper arm, which are responsible for flexing and extending the elbow, and the quadriceps muscle at the front of the thigh, which extends the knee and allows the leg

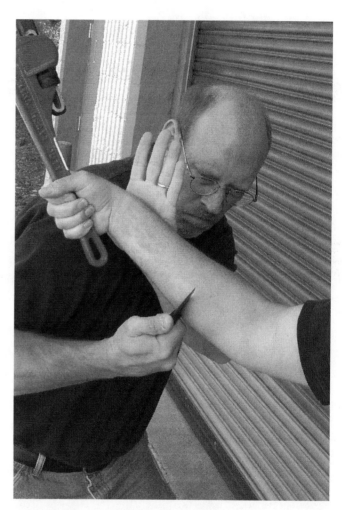

The primary target in MBC is the inner wrist and forearm of the attacker's weapon-wielding hand. Cutting the muscles and tendons of this area can immediately cripple the hand and disarm your attacker. In the Filipino martial arts, this tactic is known as "defanging the snake."

to support weight. Targeting these structures can destroy or severely inhibit the arm's ability to wield a weapon and the attacker's ability to achieve the mobility necessary to press his attack. Again, powerful, accurate cuts to these targets produce instantaneous results and greatly increase your chances of survival. The quadriceps cut, in particular, can be extremely effective since destroying your attacker's mobility (the "mobility kill" concept discussed in previous chapters) enables you to create distance, and with distance comes safety.

This practical approach to knife stopping power is the foundation of MBC's tactics. In addition to the biomechanical aspects of destroying the structures that enable an attacker to pose a threat, it also incorporates neurological targeting and typically results in serious arterial bleeding as well. This three-tiered approach to stopping power is based on the pioneering work of my late friend Chris Grosz and my own in-depth research on human anatomy and its vulnerability to edged-weapon tactics. Since developing MBC, I have taught

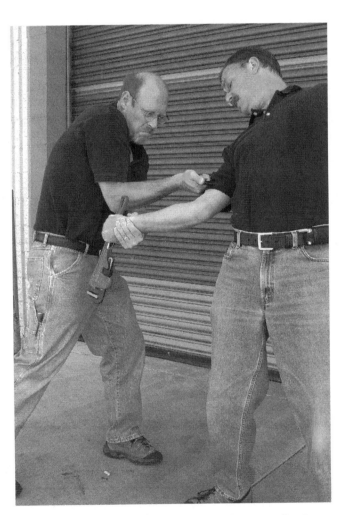

MBC's second target priority is the bicep and triceps muscles of the upper arm. They are responsible for flexing and extending the elbow joint—motions that are necessary for your attacker to wield a weapon effectively.

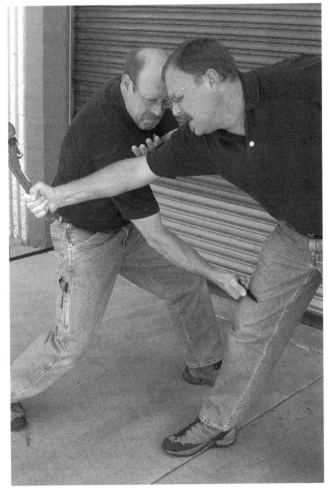

The ultimate MBC target is the quadriceps muscle—specifically the area in the first few inches above the knee. This muscle extends the knee joint and allows the leg to support weight. Severing it creates a "mobility kill," destroying or significantly inhibiting your attacker's mobility and allowing you to create distance and flee to safety.

it—and my logic of stopping power—to literally thousands of students, including dozens of medical professionals ranging from paramedics to trauma surgeons. I have also taught it at one of the world's most respected tactical medicine schools: the International School of Tactical Medicine. I'm honored to say that the doctors of that school and the other medical professionals I've taught support my logic and agree that this approach to stopping power is sound. If you practice knife-based martial arts or defensive tactics, don't rely on what history claims will work. Assess your tactics from the perspective of modern medical science and make sure they'll work.

This chapter—like the aspects of the MBC system addressed in the context of *The Best Defense* TV show—is just a brief overview of the entire system. If you're truly interested in developing practical defensive knife skills, please look into my *Martial Blade Concepts* video series, available from Say Safe Media (www.staysafemedia.com) or consult my web site (www.martialbladeconcepts.com) to seek out hands-on instruction from me or one of my qualified instructors. My web site also includes information on the MBC Distance Learning program, a comprehensive at-home self-study program in the MBC system.

CHAPTER 11: POINT SHOOTING—THE HEART OF ALL SHOOTING TECHNIQUE

Colonel Rex Applegate is a name that should be familiar to all students of combat shooting. One of the true legends of the close-combat sciences, his contributions to the field spanned more than half a century and included practically every one of its disciplines. From unarmed tactics to knife fighting to riot control, the Colonel did it all and did it exceedingly well.

But the Colonel's greatest passion—and arguably his most significant contribution—was his research and promotion of handgun point shooting.

The term "point shooting" often elicits powerful reactions from many shooters—especially those who fail to understand the fundamental elements of their own shooting technique and focus more on cliché and dogma than real skill.

My perspective of point shooting comes from in-depth analysis of the Colonel's works, but more importantly from firsthand range instruction, professional collaborations, and countless conversations during the last few years of the Colonel's life. For the record, my first introduction to Colonel Applegate's work was when I read his book *Kill or Get Killed* when I was about 13 years old. About 20 years after that, I was hired by Paladin Press (still publishers of that book and the Colonel's other works) with the specific purpose of establishing their video production department to produce point shooting videos with Colonel Applegate. In fact, my acceptance for that position was actually contingent upon the Colonel's approval; if he didn't like me, I didn't get the job.

Fortunately for me, the Colonel not only took a liking to me, he also appreciated my active interest in the history and tactics of close combat. To ensure that I could accurately express his methods in the videos we produced, he personally mentored me in point shooting and other topics. Ultimately he was pleased enough with my understanding and skill that he invited me to co-author a book on the topic with him, titled *Bullseyes Don't Shoot Back*. Needless to say, that was an incredible honor and will always remain one of the highlights of my career.

During our collaboration on that book, the Colonel shared a lot of information with me about the history and development of point shooting. However, to present the strongest case for the *modern* application of the system, he asked that we not include those details so the book could focus on the application of the technique in today's world. For the scope of that project that was appropriate, but the time has come to tell the full story.

Origins of the Applegate Technique

When Colonel Applegate was personally recruited by the legendary "Wild Bill" Donovan (director of what began as the Coordinator of Information (COI) and later became the Office of Strategic Services (OSS)), he was initially paired with another close-combat icon, William Ewart Fairbairn. With decades of experience with the Shanghai Municipal Police, Fairbairn already had a highly evolved curriculum of armed and unarmed combat to offer. That system—including the point shooting system that he developed with his Shanghai colleague Eric Anthony Sykes—therefore became a significant turnkey part of the OSS curriculum. However, it wasn't the only influence on Colonel Applegate's approach.

Those familiar with the Colonel's history know that he also conducted extensive personal research into combat shooting—including research into the methods of Western gunfighters. In the course of this study, he discovered a letter written by the legendary Wild Bill Hickok in which Hickok explained the secret of his gunfighting success. Specifically, he revealed that during his gunfights he always took the time to raise the gun to eye level before firing. That revelation really resonated with Colonel Applegate and became a key element of his preferred shooting method.

A somewhat lesser-known fact is that one of the Colonel's earliest shooting influences was his uncle, exhibition shooter Gus Peret. Like most exhibition shooters of the early 20th century, Peret had uncanny eye-hand coordination and performed feats that included both incredible kinesthetic/point shooting and the amazingly precise use of the gun's sights. Through Peret the Colonel learned at a very early age both the advantages and limitations of both approaches to shooting. He also learned that there is a huge difference between the skills of a naturally gifted shooter with an unlimited supply of practice ammo and the capabilities of the common man. That understanding would later serve him and his students very well.

When you combine these influences and compare the WWII-era Applegate technique with Fairbairn's technique, there is one major difference. While Fairbairn acknowledged that shooting from eye level was preferable, he placed a heavy emphasis on what he called the "Three-Quarter Hip" position, in which the gun hand was only raised to center-chest level. The Applegate technique, however, reflected his own research and experience and adamantly

The late Col. Rex Applegate was one of the pioneers of modern close-combat technique. His greatest contribution was in the field of handgun point shooting.

advocated raising the gun to eye level. In fact in his classic *Kill or Get Killed* he specifically warns *against* hip shooting and other below-line-of-sight methods and clearly separates the from his recommended method of combat point shooting.

The Physiological Effects of Life-Threatening Stress

Whenever we are exposed to life-threatening danger, our bodies react instinctively by activating the Sympathetic Nervous System (SNS)—an aspect of our nervous system that governs our most primal survival instincts. Overtly, we experience the "startle response," which is characterized by crouching, raising the hands, lowering the head, raising the shoulders, and facing the perceived threat squarely. Internally, our bodies react by increasing the heart rate and dilating the bronchial passages to increase athletic efficiency, stopping the digestive process to optimize blood flow, limiting blood flow to the appendages, releasing strength-increasing hormones like adrenaline, and dilating the pupils to maximize visual input. Although seasoned veterans of high-stress situations can learn to mitigate these effects—collectively known as the "Body Alarm Reaction" (BAR) or the "fight or flight" reflex—for most people they are unavoidable. And if they are the expected "norm," logically they should also be the first step in any trained combative technique.

Of these effects, pupil dilation has the most profound impact on what a shooter can actually see when faced with a threat. Just like a camera lens, the larger the aperture (the opening of the pupil), the less depth of field the eye has. According to numerous scientific studies, when the body is reacting to life-threatening stress and experiencing the BAR, the eyes are physically incapable of focusing at close range—less than about four feet. In simple terms, odds are you will not be physiologically able to see your sights.

It is also important to understand that your eyes can only focus at one distance or focal "plane" at one time. Even if you could make the visual shift from the guy that's trying to kill you to your sights, you will probably keep your eyes on him *because he's trying to kill you*.

With all this in mind, the ability to kinesthetically aim your gun at an attacker while maintaining your focus on the threat makes perfect sense. Since "tunnel vision"—the narrowing of the visual field—is also a consistent effect associated with the BAR, raising the gun to eye level so it at least appears in the line of sight also makes sense. No matter what

The author had the privilege of working very closely with Col. Applegate for several years and the honor of co-authoring a book with him. Bullseyes Don't Shoot Back is still regarded as the seminal modern reference on handgun point shooting.

shooting method you prefer, these components are critical to its functional efficiency during the stress of a defensive situation.

Thou Shalt Not Shove Thy Handgun

One characteristic element of Applegate-style point shooting is the concept of locking the wrist and elbow and raising the gun to the line of sight. The purpose of this technique is to prevent shoving the gun forward at the target—an action that when fueled by the gross motor skills of fear-induced stress causes a violent downward whip of the muzzle at full extension. Even at short ranges, this can cause rounds to impact much lower than the intended point of aim and, under extreme stress, even into the dirt in front of the target.

In all of his teaching, Colonel Applegate explained that the effects of shoving the handgun are most pronounced when the shooter begins from a muzzle-up-and-downrange ready position—unfortunately the official "safe" position for most military firearms training. However, the Colonel also confided that "raising the arm like a pump handle" also helped correct another marksmanship problem of the WWII era: the influence of films, particularly Westerns.

Since the action in Western movies focused on the use of single-action revolvers, the most familiar shooting technique to the average man at that time was to raise the muzzle, thumb cock the hammer, lower the gun, and fire. Many of the recruits that Colonel Applegate had to train were selected for skills such as such as foreign language fluency, area knowledge, etc., so they were by no means seasoned shooters. When given a handgun, they shot based on what they *thought* they knew from the movies. Just as a kid today might reflexively roll the gun over "gangsta" style or adopt a muzzle-up, cup-and-saucer "Full Sabrina" ready stance, novice shooters in WWII often tended to shoot like their heroes in the movies. The "pump handle" raise helped cure that.

Weapon Grip and Centerline

In Fairbairn and Sykes' book *Shooting to Live*, considerable attention is paid to the importance of understanding the vertical centerline of the body and making sure that the wrist of gun hand is bent slightly outward (to the right for a right-handed shooter) to align the bore with that centerline. By doing this, and following the natural instinct to turn your entire body to square up with a lethal threat, you automatically point your centerline and the gun at the target and achieve proper windage.

While Colonel Applegate's early teachings also recommend bending the wrist slightly, he placed a much heavier emphasis on the importance of bisecting the angle of the web of

Col. Applegate's preferred point shooting stance—feet spread and knees bent in a natural crouch, shoulders squared to the threat, wrist and elbow locked, and arm raised "like a pump handle" to eye level.

the thumb when assuming a grip on the gun. In fact, in *Kill or Get Killed*, he recommends that the centerline position is only mandatory *during the early stages of training*. As the shooter becomes more proficient, he can relax his technique and allow the gun to move away from centerline—as long as he's still getting acceptable hits.

During the production of the video *Shooting for Keeps* and the writing of *Bullseyes Don't Shoot Back*, I asked the Colonel about the importance of the centerline concept. Once again, he did not consider it a major factor and not nearly as important as bisecting the angle of the web of the thumb to get the weapon bore on line with the forearm. Consistent with his wishes, I did not emphasize it. However, I noticed a significant difference in the performance of the shooters who appeared in the video—one of whom used the centerline concept and the other, who did not.

In one scene, the Colonel wanted to show how ordinary paper plates not only made excellent center-mass targets for shooting practice, but how they could be easily hit with proper point shooting technique. We set up a series of plates spaced laterally and the centerline shooter—his grandson—had no problem quickly working his way down the line scoring a hit on each plate. The non-centerline shooter, who was also a law enforcement officer personally trained by the Colonel, had developed a habit of maintaining a straight wrist. Although he compensated for this like most shooters—by pulling his right shoulder back slightly—his ability to transition laterally between targets was never as good as the centerline shooter.

Years later, after the Colonel's point shooting curriculum had been officially adopted by Ohio's Hocking College and become the law enforcement training standard for many law enforcement agencies in that state, I ran into a Brazilian friend of mine who had gone through the program. He knew that I had trained with Colonel Applegate and co-authored a point shooting book and immediately said that he "had to ask me some questions about point shooting." My equally immediate response was, "Are you wondering why you shoot to the left at longer ranges?" I interpreted his stunned expression as a "yes" and proceeded to explain the subtleties of bending the gun-hand wrist to put the bore on centerline and the effects of failing to do so. Based on my research following the Colonel's death, I found that shooters with same-side gun hands and master eyes can often "cheat" the centerline concept by bringing the gun up in front of the master eye and pulling their shoulder back slightly. However, it seems

The author demonstrates Applegate-style point-shooting technique with tracer ammo. Note the locked-wrist position and the fact that the gun's boreline coincides with the axis of the forearm. This is in contrast to the centerline concept emphasized by Fairbairn.

that they still don't shoot as well when using this method to shift between laterally spaced targets.

Using Technique to Promote Combat Mindset

One of the biggest misconceptions about point shooting is that its advocates claim that it will produce the same level of accuracy as sighted fire. Colonel Applegate never claimed this and made it clear that point shooting is intended to achieve acceptable accuracy and center-mass hits in the conditions of actual combat. Curiously, he still made use of the common belief that tight groups on a two-dimensional target equates to (or at least creates the impression of) combat proficiency.

Many of the students the Colonel trained had very limited time to develop combat skills. In some cases, they only had a few hours of firearms training before they were shipped overseas. To give them the basic skills they needed and to instill confidence, they were taught point shooting at very close ranges—usually only 2-3 yards. At this distance, even novice shooters had no problem achieving good center mass groups. They also unknowingly got accustomed to operating at very close range and experiencing things like muzzle-blast overpressure. This positive experience was very empowering and did much to instill students with a proper combat mindset—an asset that is much more important in a real fight than sterile, square-range shooting skills. This type of approach was common in WWII training methods and was instrumental in developing both basic, reliable, combat skills and the fighting spirit to apply them effectively.

Colonel Applegate's version of point shooting was the perfect solution for a critical training challenge in WWII. In later years, it also served as a tremendous catalyst for change in our approach to modern combat shooting methods. This is most apparent in the gradual shift among most instructors from the bent-arm Weaver stance to the Isosceles, which extends both arms equally to square the shoulders with the threat and place the gun on the body's centerline.

Even hard-core Weaver shooters, if they think about it logically, will acknowledge that they use their stance and body position to kinesthetically align the gun with the target before either confirming or refining that alignment with the sights. In essence, they first "point" the gun before they "sight" the gun. This kinesthetic alignment is the true heart of point shooting and ultimately the core of all shooting technique.

No matter where you stand on the topic, you owe it to yourself to become familiar with the concepts and reasoning behind point shooting—most importantly the instinctive, unavoidable, physiological effects of life-threatening stress. The shooting methods shared by Rob Pincus and Mike Seeklander in the context of *The Best Defense* fully acknowledge the effects the BAR and are designed to help shooters function effectively in the stress of real defensive shooting encounters. I highly recommend their programs to anyone interested in bridging the gap between "shooting" and the methods of actual defensive "gunfighting."

I will also be producing instructional materials on my personal approach to combative shooting and the lessons I learned directly from Col. Applegate. Please consult my web site www.martialbladeconcepts.com for information on these materials.

CHAPTER 12: CARJACKING DEFENSES

Carjacking is one of the most terrifying crimes you could ever imagine. Unlike a car thief, who wants your vehicle but really wants nothing to do with you, a carjacker *wants* to interact with you. And to do that, he is typically ready and willing to use violence. That fact, combined with the speed and surprise with which most carjackings occur, make it an incredibly difficult crime to defend against.

Fortunately, like most crimes, there is a lot you can do to prevent carjacking. The more alert and aware you are—and the more precautions you can work into your daily habits—the safer you can be.

Carjacking Basics

The first thing you need to understand and accept about carjacking is that your car is NOT worth dying for. To a carjacker, however, it may be worth killing for. Even if you are aware and avoidant, it's possible that you can be caught "behind the curve" by a carjacker. If that happens, remember that safe escape is always the ultimate victory. Give up your keys and escape.

Carjackings typically happen in one of two ways: Either the carjacker approaches you as you enter or exit your car, or he approaches you while you are behind the wheel and your vehicle is stopped. Let's deal with these in order.

Anytime you are approaching or exiting your vehicle, you are "out in public." That means that all the principles of awareness, avoidance, de-escalation, and boundary setting should be in full effect. If they are not, you need to go back and review those and make sure that you cultivate the proper level of awareness anytime you are in public.

Approaching and Entering Your Vehicle Safely

Once you have reviewed the basics of awareness, the next step in your planning should be to become familiar with some of the specific things that you should look for when you are approaching your parked vehicle. The potential signs of danger that you should be looking for include:

- People loitering around your car (especially if they react in some way when you approach)
- People sitting in nearby parked vehicles

- Vehicles following you or cruising the parking lot
- Possible hiding places near your vehicle, including vans and vehicles with tinted windows
- Anyone hiding beside, behind, under, or in your car—look before you get in

If you see something that concerns you, stop and keep distance on your side. *Do not* walk into a situation that makes you uncomfortable. If possible, go back and ask parking lot security or a friend to escort you to your car.

You should also ensure that you are prepared to enter your car efficiently and be able to drive away in a timely manner. The longer you linger in your vehicle, the more vulnerable you are. The tactics that you can adopt to help you achieve this include:

- Have your keys ready in your hand *before* you approach your car. Ideally, they should be in your weak hand, leaving your strong hand free to draw the weapon or weapons you should be carrying, or at least to strike empty handed.
- Carry any bags or other objects in your weak hand, again to leave your strong hand free. If you must carry something with two hands, be prepared to drop it if you have to defend yourself.
- If you carry a "bridging" weapon (an improvised or innocuous purpose-designed weapon that you can use as an immediate response to a threat), have it prepositioned in your strong hand. A flashlight is ideal for this purpose since it allows you better visibility in low light conditions and reminds you to be aware.
- Use electronic key locks whenever possible. Only unlock the driver's side door if you are alone to prevent anyone lurking nearby from entering your vehicle through another door.
- Know how to use the panic button on your electronic key. If you see signs of danger and cannot either escape or enter your car quickly, activate the alarm to call attention to your situation.
- Keep separate key rings for each car you drive and for your home and carry only the keys you need in your hand. That way if you are forced to surrender your keys, you surrender only the keys to that vehicle—not the keys to your home and everything else you own. Since the carjacker will have your car registration, he will also have your address, so this is an important safeguard.
- Keep your head up and continue scanning as you unlock your car and stay alert as you

Keep your car keys on a separate key ring from your house keys. If you are the victim of a carjacking, you can give up your car without giving the criminal easy access to your house and the rest of your life.

Carjacking Defenses

enter your vehicle. If you must put packages or other items in your car, do so quickly and efficiently and maintain your awareness of the environment as you do so.
- Once you are in your vehicle, *lock your doors, keep the windows up*, and put on your seatbelt as you continue to use your mirrors to scan the area around you. Then, start the car and get moving.
- If you notice anything stuck to your windows (like a notice or sticker on the back window), *do not* get out of the vehicle. Drive away and deal with it somewhere else. This is a common ploy used by carjackers to get people to exit their cars while they are running, leaving them very vulnerable to an attack.

Exiting Your Vehicle Safely

Exiting your vehicle can also be a time of vulnerability to carjacking. Some carjackers prefer to catch people unaware as they get out of their vehicles and before they "tune in" to their surroundings. Again, by keeping your head in the game and taking the time to apply a few simple tactics, you can significantly reduce your risk of falling victim to this type of attack. The recommended tactics for exiting your vehicle safely include:

- Whenever possible, back into the parking space or look for pull-through spots that allow you to drive forward to exit. This makes it much easier to drive away quickly if necessary.
- Park under or near lights in areas that allow you good visibility and avenues of escape.
- Stay away from parking areas that offer concealment (like those near walls, dumpsters, and similar objects)
- Before you unlock your doors and get out of your vehicle, take a moment to look around. If you see any causes for concern or things don't feel right, drive away and park somewhere else.
- When you're ready to get out, release your seatbelt, get whatever you need to take with you, organize yourself, and *then* unlock the doors.
- As you get out, scan the area and tune up your awareness. Be prepared to react.
- Keep your key in your hand in case you need to activate the panic button or, in a worst-case scenario, surrender it.
- Once you have decided to move away from your vehicle, lock all the doors (don't forget the trunk or hatchback) and take note of its location. This will help you approach it directly when you return so you are not wandering aimlessly in the parking lot.
- Never leave your vehicle running when unattended and never leave your keys in the vehicle.

Avoiding Carjacking while Driving

The other primary method used by carjackers is to attack you while you are behind the wheel of your vehicle. In most cases, this occurs when you are stopped at a stoplight or otherwise "boxed in" and either unable or reluctant to drive away. Depending upon the access that you allow them, they can threaten you with a weapon, physically attack you, or simply pull you out of the vehicle.

To keep yourself safe from this type of attack, you need to follow two fundamental tactics: make full use of all the physical security your car offers and always maintain the option and ability to drive away from danger.

The more physical barriers you can put between you and a potential carjacker, the safer you will be. The tactics for doing this include:

- Keep all your car doors locked whenever you are in your vehicle.
- Keep your keys in the ignition and be prepared to start the car quickly and drive away if necessary.
- Wear your seatbelt. This not only keeps you safer in the event of an accident, it is actually a deterrent to some carjackers because it makes you more difficult to pull out of the vehicle quickly.
- In warm weather, use your air conditioning and do not roll down your windows. If

you do not have air conditioning, roll your windows down only slightly—not enough to allow someone to reach in to grab or strike you or to unlock your doors.

The other aspect of avoiding a carjacking when you are in your vehicle involves your driving habits. By adjusting the way you drive, you can make yourself a much harder target and preserve your best defense against this type of attack—driving away. Here are the critical tactics that you should apply anytime you are operating a vehicle:

- Remember, the basic rule when you are behind the wheel is, "When in doubt, DRIVE." The easiest and most effective way to escape danger and call attention to your situation is by stepping on the gas. Remember this and remind yourself of it often, so if something does happen, you won't hesitate to act.
- Research the areas you drive through and know their reputations. Avoid driving in high crime areas or areas where carjackings are common.
- When driving in traffic, always leave enough room so you can see the rear tires of the car in front of you. If you can see the tires of the car in front of you, you should have the turning radius to be able to drive around that car if necessary. If you pull too close, it is easy to be boxed in and be unable to drive away.
- Whenever practical, drive in the left lane or passing lane. This keeps you away from the curb side of the street, which makes it harder for someone to approach your car (he has to cross a lane of traffic to do so) and makes it easier to see an approach sooner.
- Learn to use your mirrors and develop the habit of using them often—both when you are moving and when you are stopped. Supplement your standard flat mirrors with stick-on parabolic mirrors or extended rear-view mirrors that allow you greater fields of view and cover your blind spots. The better you can see, the more aware you can be.
- Driving away from the danger of a carjacker may include jumping curbs, ramming the vehicle in front of you, or taking other actions that you would not normally consider. Consider them now and plan for them. Better still, take a course in evasive driving and really learn how to drive away from danger. The investment in that training is money well spent.

Carjackings happen suddenly, viciously, and without warning. Stay alert and always be prepared to drive away from danger.

Carjacking Defenses

- Never open your window to talk to anyone who approaches your car on foot. If you do feel compelled to speak to someone through your window, lower it only slightly (not enough for someone to reach in and unlock your door or grab you) and be prepared to drive away at the slightest sign of trouble.
- Pre-plan your reactions based on who's in the car with you. For example, if you are alone, you have the option to flee the car if necessary; however, with a baby in a car seat, that's no longer a viable option. You'll need to adjust your reaction plan accordingly.
- If all else fails and a carjacker gets the jump on you, never go anywhere with him. Make it clear that you're giving him the vehicle, get out, and move to safety. Try to remember as many details of his appearance of possible and be a good witness, but never allow yourself to be taken to another location.
- Invest in theft insurance and Lo-Jack or a similar GPS tracking and recovery system. Such systems are by no means a replacement for awareness and avoidance tactics, but they can greatly increase the chances of recovering your vehicle.

The best defense against carjacking is to drive away. In traffic, always stay far enough behind the vehicle in front of you so you can see its rear tires. That means you have enough room to maneuver around it to drive away—even if it means jumping a curb.

In-Car Defense—Non-Firearm

Attempting to fight a carjacker inside a vehicle is a last-ditch effort, especially with any type of contact-distance weapon. More importantly, such a tactic implies that you would let down your guard by violating all the tactics of physical security that we discussed earlier—a major mistake. Although it's not wrong to prepare for the possibility that you might have to fight inside your car, it's smarter to spend more time on developing security habits that will help prevent that from being necessary.

The confined space inside a car makes it extremely difficult to maneuver. And without room to maneuver, your strikes will typically lack power and effectiveness. Even if you do manage to hit with significant power, unless that strike either persuades or propels your attacker out of the car, you still have a serious problem on your hands.

In-car defenses also require that whatever weapon you plan to use is immediately available to you and can be drawn and employed with extreme speed. If it can't, it's not going to do you much good if you suddenly find an unwanted companion in your car.

For the sake of argument—and to give you a fighting chance should you ever have to defend yourself inside a vehicle—here are a few things to consider:

- If you are surprised by an attacker who approaches your car when your window is down, release your seat belt, pivot to face the window, lean back, and get your hands up. Use verbal skills to create the opportunity to roll up your window and drive away.
- If someone reaches through your open window to grab you, try to pivot and create distance as described above. Grab his fingers if possible and wrench them quickly and ruthlessly to break them. Do not try to apply gradual pressure or "submit" him—hurt him and get away.
- If someone gets in the seat next to you, again, pivot to face him and get your hands

up. If your car's configuration and your physical abilities allow it, use your legs to kick him and force him out of the car. Be careful as you do so that you do not leave yourself vulnerable to grabs and strikes from behind.
- It is a good idea to stage some type of weapon in your car that you can access and employ quickly. Some examples of potent improvised weapons that you can easily—and legally—position in your car include an ice scraper tucked into seat next to you, a pen or tactical flashlight in center console or visor, or a screwdriver or similar tool positioned within easy reach.
- Understand the limits of your range of motion and ability to generate power inside the car and develop basic weapon skills for that environment. You'll find that reverse-grip, hammer-like strikes usually work best, especially when you target the parts he "gives" you or can't defend very well, like the hands, legs, and groin. The eyes and throat are excellent targets and certainly worth attacking, but they are more readily defended and harder to hit.
- If you do manage to injure or stun your attacker but he doesn't get out of the vehicle, consider grabbing your keys and leaving the vehicle. Obviously, you would only want to do this if you can quickly escape to a public place or other safe area. You would not want to get out of your vehicle and step into a worse situation that you faced inside it—including having to deal with all your carjacker's friends.
- If the carjacker has a gun—unless you are absolutely convinced that he's going to shoot you—give him the car and escape. Attempting a disarm in a vehicle is extremely risky and your odds of succeeding are slim.

Carjacking is a terrifying crime and defending against it is extremely difficult. Although an investment in developing your skills of awareness and avoidance always goes a long way toward ensuring your safety, this is particularly so when it comes to preventing carjacking. Make a concerted effort, change your habits, and keep your options of escape open. That's truly your best defense.

CHAPTER 13: WORKPLACE VIOLENCE

According to the U.S. Labor Department's Census of Fatal Occupational Injuries, homicide is now the third leading cause of occupational death for all workers, exceeded only by motor-vehicle incidents and falls. Based on studies of the period 1993-1999, roughly 1.7 million U.S. workers are victimized by workplace violence each year, a rate of 13 incidents for every 1,000 employees. In simple terms, the threat of workplace violence is very real. Unfortunately, most of the efforts to address this growing problem actually do very little to protect you from becoming a victim.

The first step in developing any type of personal protection program is accepting the fact that you are the only one who can keep yourself safe. Although security guards, metal detectors, and corporate policies help, the reality of the situation is that if someone is truly determined to commit workplace violence, he or she will. Like all crimes, it is a matter of intent, not materiel. Once you have accepted that, your next step should be to figure out what you can do about it and what measures you can take to ensure your safety.

Evaluate "The System"

Because workplace violence has become so common, most businesses have taken some measures to prevent it. As a concerned employee, your first step should therefore be to objectively assess what your company has done and determine what level of protection it provides. What type of physical security do they have to restrict unauthorized access? Do they employ security personnel? If so, are they armed and, more importantly, are they skilled in using those weapons? Is there a policy that prohibits the carry or possession of weapons on the company grounds and, if so, what procedures are used to enforce it?

In addition to researching the answers to these questions, you should also do a critical assessment from the perpetrator's point of view. If you were a disgruntled employee with vengeance on your mind, could you enter the building if you wanted to? Could you introduce a firearm or other weapon into the workplace without being detected? And if you behaved violently, could anyone effectively stop you?

If you're like most people, you'll find that the institutional security of your business leaves a lot to be desired. Once again, you've confirmed that you're on your own.

Your Area's Physical Security

The next step should be to consider the physical security of your specific workplace and what you can do to improve it. If you have an office, take a hard look at the door and the lock and decide whether they really qualify as an effective barrier. If they are sound, are there other structural weaknesses, like windows, that could be easily breached? In basic terms, decide whether your immediate workplace could be used as a "safe room" to survive a workplace attack.

If the physical security of the room itself is adequate, your next step should be to identify any ballistic cover (structures or objects that will actually stop bullets) in your area. If you actually have things like brick walls and concrete pillars to work with, take a hard look at them from a potential shooter's perspective. If your office was locked and someone was firing in at you, what angles and fields of fire would they have and how could you use the available cover in your office most effectively?

Based on that knowledge, it's now time to do some "tactical redecorating." Configure your office to make the best use of the available cover and ensure that you have the greatest possible visibility of anyone approaching your office. Turn your desk to face the most likely avenues of entry and, if necessary, place mirrors, pictures, or other reflective objects to maximize your ability to see people approaching you from all angles.

If you don't have structural cover to work with, create your own. Books and similar forms of densely packed paper are excellent bullet stoppers. By strategically placing a few bookshelves and filing cabinets in your office, you can create some very effective sources of cover. Filing cabinets can be made even more effective by placing a few old phonebooks or thick textbooks in the back of every drawer. It's not perfect, but it's certainly better than nothing.

"Universal" Door Locks

Many businesses have offices that feature sturdy interior doors that do not lock or have substandard locks that don't provide an adequate barrier to violent entry. If the door of your office is solid, but doesn't lock well, ask your employer if you can install a quality lock and reinforced strike plate at your own expense. If he won't let you, but the knob on your door is the sturdy industrial type, invest in an adjustable security bar. This is a strong, tubular-steel device with a

In addition to arming yourself (if possible), you should also configure your office to make the best use of cover. A heavy wooden desk can be made even better by filling drawers with phonebooks, thick hardcover books, or similar materials. Your dry fire and range training should also include "training in context" to allow you to practice shooting from these unconventional positions.

non-slip rubber foot and a cradle that fits under the doorknob. Place the cradle under the knob, kick the foot to wedge it securely in place, and you've got an instant lock.

An alternate—or supplemental—approach is to make a couple of sturdy hardwood door stops. Cover the contact surfaces with skateboard tape or rubber stair-tread tape to prevent slipping and drill a hole through the wide end for a strong loop of cord. If you hear gunshots down the hall and need to hunker down, close your door and use a hammer to drive the doorstops securely under the door. When it's safe—or at least preferable—to leave, slide the hammer handle through the cord loops and use it to pull the stops out.

Why would you have a hammer in your office? Because weapons—especially those that don't look like weapons—should also be part of your plan.

Weapons Are in the Eye of the Beholder

Being well armed is always a good thing. If you can get a concealed carry permit in your state, do it. If you can extend that carry into your workplace to ensure that you have a firearm available to you at all times, do that too. Unfortunately, many companies have adopted no-weapons policies that have effectively turned their facilities into "non-permissive" environments—at least for people who play by the rules. Obviously, a co-worker or customer who is mentally unstable enough to commit a violent assault isn't going to think twice about the technicalities of violating a weapon policy, so, as with the rest of society, weapons restrictions only disarm the law abiding.

If your workplace does not have any *physical* measures (i.e., metal detectors) to prevent you from carrying a weapon, you certainly could choose to carry or store a weapon in your office. That decision—and acceptance of the potential consequences that come with it—is of course up to you.

A lower-profile approach, however, is to equip your work area with tools or other items that also have significant potential as weapons. Bring in a hammer to hang a few pictures and forget to take it home. Start collecting scissors and letter openers. Bring leftover steak for lunch—and a steak knife with which to cut it. Develop a sudden interest in baseball and display an autographed "collectible" bat (even if you have to autograph it yourself). And, very importantly, buy your own dry chemical fire extinguisher that you maintain in your office.

Obviously a hammer, pair of scissors, steak knife, or even a baseball bat isn't the preferred

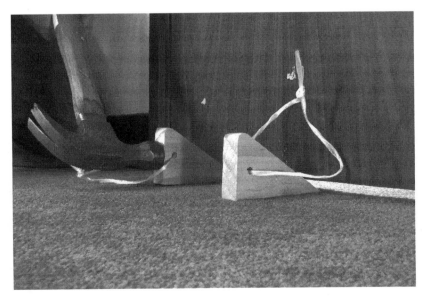

If you work in an office that does not have a locking door, one way to secure it in the event of a workplace violence incident is to use wooden door stops. Prepared in advance and kept readily accessible with a hammer (to hammer them into place and serve as a weapon), they can turn an ordinary door into a life-saving physical barrier.

weapon against an attacker armed with a firearm, but they're better than nothing. As for the fire extinguisher, it qualifies as both a distance weapon and an impact weapon. Against an armed attacker, spray the chemical into his face and eyes to blind him, and then beat him unconscious with the body of the extinguisher.

The exact tools/weapons you choose will depend upon the non-permissive environment in which you work and how far you can stretch the rules of plausible deniability. Whatever you choose, make sure you have a real, workable plan and keep your weapons ready and available at all times. Critical incidents happen quickly, so make sure you can react just as quickly if you need to.

No Safe Haven

So far, we've been operating based on the assumption that your workplace also has the physical structure to serve as a safe room—a place where you can lock yourself in and weather the storm. Unfortunately, many people don't have that luxury. If you work in an open area, a cubicle, or any other place that doesn't support safe-room tactics, hunkering down is not your best bet. Your strategy should be based on recognizing and, if necessary, withstanding the initial assault, followed by immediate escape.

To best recognize and weather the initial attack, you'll need to have good visibility of the surrounding area and, if possible, some form of cover between you and the most likely fields of fire. The process for doing this is exactly the same as if you had a dedicated office, albeit more challenging. Arrange your work area to provide visibility, use reflective surfaces to compensate for blind spots and increase fields of vision, and, if possible, position things like filing cabinets to provide some degree of ballistic cover. Having a weapon can significantly improve your chances of survival, so use the same strategies discussed earlier to ensure that you have one or more available to you at all times.

Once you've made your work area as survivable as possible, it's time to start planning your escape routes. The best way to do this is to again view your environment through the eyes of the bad guy. First, determine the most likely entrance he would use and who he would encounter there. If we assume that he starts shooting at that point, what cover or concealment separates you from him? What other exits are available to you at that time? And, very importantly, what sources of cover are available to you on the route from your work area to the other exits? In basic terms, your goal is to immediately identify the location of the

One of the best improvised weapons in a non-permissive environment is a dry chemical fire extinguisher. It can be used to blind an attacker from a significant distance and as a potent impact weapon.

threat and exit the area by leapfrogging from cover to cover so you're as safe as possible along the way.

Your primary escape route should be based on the path that provides the safest, most efficient escape from the most likely type of attack. However, it shouldn't be your only plan. Have at least one, preferably more, alternate routes in the event your primary route is blocked or unusable. Also, war game potential scenarios based on different threat locations and decide in advance when an alternate route should become a primary one because the situation has changed.

Practice Makes Perfect

When you have all those routes straight in your head, your next step should be to validate them by actually walking through them and taking them to a logical conclusion. Look for any potential barriers or obstacles like locked doors and make your theories into real workable plans. Then, practice them on a regular basis to make them an ingrained response. Your practice doesn't need to be elaborate or alarming to anyone—just a physical rehearsal and reinforcement of your mental plans.

The final step in your escape plans should be to arrive at a conclusive end or goal. Don't just be content to get out of the building; escape to a specific location where you are safe and have the ability to contact the police and report the incident. Also, have a plan to contact family members, co-workers, and anyone else who might be concerned about your safety when news of the incident becomes public. They will definitely appreciate early notice of your status.

Workplace violence is a real threat in today's world. And like any other form of self-protection, the key to being prepared for it is to accept the reality of the threat and take tangible, logical steps to develop your own response plans. And, remember, the best thing about being on your own is that you know exactly who you can trust.

CHAPTER 14: SELF-DEFENSE FOR THE PHYSICALLY CHALLENGED

Personal protection is, as the name implies, a very personal thing. Although many instructors will claim that their system, their secret technique, or their weapon of choice will allow anyone to defeat even the biggest attacker, it's not that easy. Like it or not, your ability to defend yourself will always be based on a dynamic combination of your tools, your skills, and the physical attributes you have to express those skills.

While this problem affects all of us, it is of particular concern to those who, for whatever reason, are not fully physically able. Whether that disability is due to a temporary injury, age, or a permanent medical condition, it defines the limits of what you can and can't do in a self-defense situation.

The bottom line is that there simply is no one-size-fits-all solution to self-defense, especially for those with physical disabilities. However, by following a logical process of self-assessment, research, planning, and training, you can create a customized set of self-defense skills and tactics that works reliably for you.

What's the Goal?

Before you start selecting weapons or planning tactics, it's a good idea to remind yourself of the actual goal in personal protection: to keep yourself and your loved ones safe, period. It is not about winning fights, teaching the bad guy a lesson, or doing society a favor. Ideally, it means that you recognize and avoid problems before they happen. If you can't avoid them, you use non-physical skills like verbalization to talk your way out of a situation. And throughout the entire process, you ensure that your brain is always stronger and smarter than your ego.

If you are forced to use physical skills to defend yourself, remember that your objective is to stop your attacker and create an opportunity for you to escape safely.

By focusing on doing whatever is necessary to stay safe, you take a proactive approach rather than a reactive one (That's why "personal protection" is a better term than "self-defense.") and learn to exercise your options earlier in the process. And the sooner you start, the more options you have.

Self-Assessment

With that goal defined, the next step is to take an honest look at your physical abilities. Focus on your abilities, not your disabilities, and really try to quantify what you're capable of. Use that assessment to objectively define your physical resources. Some questions that you might ask yourself include:

- How fast and how far can I walk or run if I had to?
- Can I stand without artificial support and wield a weapon?
- How hard can I hit with a weapon like a stick or cane?
- Can I stand without artificial support and strike with my hands and elbows?
- Can I kick?
- Do I have the strength and dexterity to shoot and manipulate a handgun?
- Can I shoot a handgun with both hands? With one hand?
- How good is my vision?
- What types of mobility aids or equipment must I use regularly?
- Do these mobility aids or equipment offer potential as improvised weapons?
- If I use a mobility aid or a wheelchair, how quickly can I move and how far can I go before stopping?

What Tools Do You Have to Work With?

Based on these questions and any others that you find relevant, you should develop a realistic understanding of what you can actually do in a personal-defense situation. These are your capabilities. With them defined, the next step should be to research the laws in your area (both state and municipality) and determine what types of weapons are legal to carry and use in self-defense. If you travel frequently, you should also research the laws in the areas you travel to and through to see how they compare to the area where you live. Ideally, your goal is to develop a list of weapons that is legally permissible in all the areas you live and operate. If the laws differ considerably, make separate lists of what is legal in each area. In that process, ensure that you include both lethal and less-lethal weapons so you have as broad a scope of use-of-force options as possible. These weapons are your potential personal-defense tools.

Wargaming: Considering Your Options in Context

With an honest understanding of your capabilities and the tools available to you, it's time to start "wargaming." Wargaming is the mental exercise of imagining plausible personal-defense situations and working through them mentally to determine practical responses. During this process, above all else, be realistic. Do not assume that you will be able to be faster, stronger, or more capable than you are now. Although adrenaline may provide some help to extend your abilities, don't count on it. Instead, plan on working with what you have based on the capabilities and resources you've already defined.

During the wargaming process, don't focus only on worst-case scenarios that would justify the use of firearms. Make sure that you consider the full scope of potential threats you might face, including everything from a belligerent drunk or aggressive panhandler through unarmed attacks and up to committed, lethal-force attacks. As you consider each situation, think of all the tools you could potentially have available to you and how they would apply. Start at the low end and evaluate your ability to recognize the situation early and, if possible, avoid it or escape it. From there, work up to verbal de-escalation and boundary setting. Finally, progress to physical skills that include unarmed tactics, less-lethal weapons, and ultimately lethal weapons.

During the initial phases of wargaming, focus on what you would do if you had a particular weapon at hand. Think about your ability to use that weapon to decisively stop your attacker, what you would do if there were multiple attackers, and how, if possible, you would escape to safety. Done honestly and objectively, this process should allow you to determine the reasonable limits of what you *could* do if the right tools were available. Based on that, the next step is to temper "ideal" with "practical" and start thinking about weapon carry and deployment.

Self-defense for the Physically Challenged

Weapon Deployment

Your physical limitations will also have a significant bearing on what weapons you can carry comfortably and how you can get them into action. For an able-bodied person, the first step in choosing a carry strategy should be to look at the way he or she typically dresses on a daily basis, as well as his or her normal daily activities. Based on that assessment and the "common ground" that it identifies, the choices of practical carry style and position begin to become apparent. For a person with a physical disability, the same process applies; however, it must also include any mobility aids, special equipment, or other daily requirements that are relevant to your personal situation. Like your mode of dress, these items define your daily "kit" and offer either advantages or disadvantages when it comes to weapon carry.

You should also consider your strength, flexibility, and range of movement when assessing your carry and deployment options, since they will also be major factors in determining which carry positions work well for you.

Learn by Example

To give you a better idea of how this whole process works, let's take a look at a representative example. Let's say that you have some type of medical condition that makes it necessary for you to walk with a cane. Whether it's a temporary or permanent condition is irrelevant; you just know that you need it to get around. With that in mind, you should first consider how well you can move with the cane. In simple terms, if you were threatened and had the opportunity to escape, could you? If possible, try to estimate how far you could go and how fast. That information will help you determine your response tactics.

Next, you should determine whether the cane represents a viable contact-distance weapon for you. Can you maintain your balance well enough without the cane to wield it as a weapon? If so, do you have the strength and coordination to wield it well enough to consider it a practical weapon? If the answers to these questions are "yes," the cane is a viable weapon and should be included in your personal-defense strategy. The fact that it, by nature, is in-hand when you are using it also makes it an excellent first line of defense, since the issues of carry, concealment, and draw stroke don't apply.

If you can't maintain your balance without the cane or don't have the physical strength and coordination to wield it with power, you must choose another path. Although potentially lethal, the cane as a weapon really represents a less-lethal option. Since you'll be using it exclusively as a mobility aid, you need to find another option to fill the less-lethal need. One excellent choice—provided it's legal in your area—would be pepper spray. Properly employed, it would give you the ability to deal with a non-life-threatening attack very effectively. It also has the potential to stop an attacker decisively enough to allow you to escape—even with limited mobility.

If possible, you should also have a lethal-force option at your disposal. A knife is certainly a possibility, but again you must have the physical ability to employ it effectively. If you do, it's another potential layer of your defense. If you don't—or even if you do—a firearm is the next logical step. If concealed carry is a legal option in your area, it's time for some more self assessment. Can you maintain your balance well enough without your cane to shoot the gun two handed? If not, are there other viable shooting positions that you can use effectively? If you need to use the cane to maintain your balance, can you shoot effectively with only one hand? If so, what size and caliber of gun will allow you to stop a threat effectively without exceeding your ability to control recoil?

As you go down this path of decision making, you should also think about the other aspects of defensive firearms use and how they apply to your situation. For example, if you must use the cane to maintain your balance, you must shoot with one hand. That means that reloading will

The Best Defense

This sequence demonstrates the thought and planning necessary to tailor your tactics to fit your physical limitations. If you use a cane for mobility, but can maintain your balance without it, it can be a viable weapon for you. Confronted by an attacker armed with a knife, the author uses the cane as an initial response, thrusting to the attacker's chest to keep him from closing and then to his groin. These hits provide the time and opportunity to then draw a gun. Switching the cane to his left hand, the author draws a J-Frame revolver from his front pocket and is prepared to follow up as necessary.

be more challenging because your "off" hand is encumbered, so a high-capacity semi-auto might be a better choice than a revolver or auto with a limited magazine capacity.

Carry Options and Your Personal Tactics

If you are right handed and have a bad right leg, doctors would advise you to use a cane with your left hand. If forced to defend yourself, your right hand would be free to draw and shoot. However, if you have a bad left leg, the cane would start in your right hand. To draw, you'd have to pass it to your left hand, stabilize your balance, and then draw. This same process would also apply if you were deploying pepper spray, a knife, or any other weapon instead of a gun. Thinking through this process as it applies to you, your specific physical condition, and your choice of weapons is the next piece of the puzzle. It's also what will allow you to realistically plan and integrate your carry strategies for your preferred weapons.

When it comes to carry and deployment, remember that your situation may be dynamic and require you to integrate your use of weapons. You may strike an attacker with your cane to create an opportunity to draw your pepper spray or gun. You may spray one attacker and be forced to shoot another. To consider all these options, go back to wargaming and incorporate carry, deployment, and transitions into your response-planning process.

Personal protection is up to the individual. If you have a physical disability, use the logic in this article to develop a plan that works for your specific needs. That's your key to staying safe.

The Best Defense

CHAPTER 15: SAFETY IN THE BACK COUNTRY

Defending yourself in an urban environment can be incredibly frightening. But believe it or not, defending yourself in the back country can be even more terrifying. To put it bluntly, the further you get from civilization, the less civilized people can become. In fact, some of the most heinous crimes ever committed took place on back country trails and in remote areas—far from witnesses and help.

Being out in the wilderness—or at least what many people regard as wilderness—can easily lull you into a state of complacency. Natural surroundings make you think that you're "away" from crime and that there's nothing to worry about. This is particularly true of seemingly remote areas, trail heads, and camp grounds that appear to be isolated, but are actually within easy reach of expressways or urban areas.

Remember, a big part of self-protection is accepting the fact that, when something happens, you're on your own—at least initially. In the city, you might be able to deal with a situation initially, and then escape to a public area that provides a degree of safety. You can also mount an initial defense and then call 911 and wait for the cavalry to arrive. In the back country these kinds of solutions probably won't be possible. Even if you do establish contact with someone, it may be a long time before they can reach you to provide help—if they can even find your exact location.

So what does this all mean? It means that when you are operating in the back country, you need to be just as aware and avoidant as you are in urban areas and, ideally, even better armed. That way you can truly increase your odds of being able to end a fight that someone else starts.

From an awareness standpoint, your first job should be to research the areas you'd like to visit before you go there. Check for reports of criminal activity, gang presence, sexual assault, and any other causes for concern before you decide to visit any wilderness area. Search Internet news and map sites to determine the crime histories of the areas you'd like to visit and their proximity to populated areas, expressway rest stops, and other potential staging areas for criminal activity. It's also a good idea to check cell phone coverage in that area (although the coverage maps may still not be definitive) so you can know in advance if you're likely to have service when you get there. Don't rely on something that you may likely be without.

Awareness also means understanding how the back country rules differ from the rules you must normally follow in the city and what other threats you might face. For example, you may not be allowed to carry a firearm in an urban area, but may be free to do so in the area you plan to visit. By the same token, the firearm and load that might be appropriate for a two-legged predator on the street may not be adequate for the four-legged ones that may prowl in your back country area of choice. Do your homework and plan accordingly.

One back country weapon that is particularly useful is a walking stick or staff. In addition to helping you negotiate rough terrain, it literally allows you to keep a potent weapon in your hand at all times. The tactics for its use are exactly the same as the cane tactics addressed elsewhere in this book.

Just as in an urban environment, awareness and the identification of potential threats should lead to avoidance. You should make every effort to steer clear of any potentially dangerous situation and proactively put as much distance between you and possible threats as possible. In the process, you need to remember that if you do not avoid a situation and are forced to react to a threat, escaping is much more difficult in the wilderness for a number of reasons. Odds are that the terrain will be challenging and it will be difficult to run away quickly. There are also fewer places to run to and you might find yourself having to run a great distance to improve your situation significantly—especially if the threat is more fit or better suited to running than you are. Finally, even if you manage to escape an immediate threat, you are still in the wilderness, far from help, and on your own. You must also understand that and prepare accordingly.

If you spend a lot of time in the wilderness, you should invest the time and effort to prepare yourself accordingly. And the best resource for that is Michael Bane's book *Trail Safe*. It focuses exclusively on the topic of back country safety and draws from Bane's extensive personal experience on the subject. It is a reference that every outdoor enthusiast should have in his or her library.

One of the best weapons in the back country is a hiking staff. Since it's carried in the hand, it is always immediately available and can be wielded with the same tactics as a cane. With only minimal training, it can become an extremely potent defensive weapon.

CONCLUSION

Self-defense—or to be more technically accurate—personal protection, is a complicated topic. Because by nature it is a very individualized thing, there is no one-size-fits-all solution. In addition to the fact that we all have different, often constantly changing physical abilities, the tactics and techniques we can employ to defend ourselves are also defined by the laws in the areas where we live and travel. What's appropriate for one person in one place may not work for that person's next-door neighbor or even that same person operating in a different area.

In writing this book, I've tried to provide a comprehensive, realistic look at the types of threats we face and the tools and skill sets available to us to deal with those threats. Your ultimate goal in reading and digesting it should be to take a critical look at your personal situation and to fill the gaps in your own defenses. Consider the broad range of threats you might encounter and honestly assess your current skills and abilities to defend against all of them. If you do find a vulnerability, invest in the training you need to fill that gap.

No matter who you are or where you live, remember that the "soft skills" of awareness, avoidance, de-escalation, and boundary setting always apply. These universal skills should not only be your first line of defense, they should also complement everything else you do to keep yourself and your family safe and should be seamlessly integrated into all your other training.

One of the favorite sayings I use when I teach is "You don't have to fight like me; you just have to fight well." I hope you enjoyed this book and that it will help you to develop the ability to fight well on your terms. Train hard, and stay safe.

RESOURCES FOR FURTHER STUDY

If you found the information in this book helpful in your personal-protection education, I urge you to explore these other learning resources.

MartialBladeConcepts.com – This is my web site and ground zero for information related to the various self-defense disciplines I teach, my seminar schedule, my most recent articles and media appearances, contact information for the instructors in my network, and many other related topics. The book and video page of the site contains information concerning the many other books I've written and the instructional videos I've produced, as well as links to order them. As the site evolves, it will also contain information on my Distance Learning Programs and other specialized instructional materials. Please bookmark it and visit it often.

StaySafeMedia.com – Stay Safe Media is both the production company and official source of all my most current mainstream instructional videos in both DVD and downloadable format. Operated by certified MBC instructor Michael Rigg, it is also the source for carefully selected personal-defense materials from other publishers and a variety of handpicked products, including limited-edition knives, training knives, and branded items featuring my MBC logo.

ICETraining.us – This is the home page for Rob Pincus' I.C.E. Training services, as well as a connection to Rob's many other programs and activities. It provides information and schedules on Combat Focus Shooting courses, instructional books and DVDs, and many other topics related to personal defense. I recommend it and Rob's instruction highly.

Shooting-Performance.com – This web site is home to Mike Seeklander's aptly named training company, Shooting-Performance. A former Federal Air Marshal and a nationally ranked shooting competitor, Mike's comprehensive knowledge of both defensive skills and tactics and cutting-edge competitive shooting shines through in all his training. His web site provides complete information on his courses, books, videos, and other activities. No matter what your personal training goals are, the resources he provides will help you achieve them.

Kembativz.com – Kelly McCann is hands down the most extraordinary instructor I've ever seen. A former U.S. Marine Corps infantry and special missions officer, his incredible breadth of knowledge includes everything from unarmed personal-defense through state-of-the-art counterterrorist tactics. He and his company, the Crucible, are the go-to sources for U.S. government agencies and Fortune 500 companies seeking the very best in specialized security training. For years, McCann's training was only offered to elite clients, but he recently made key aspects of his training curriculum available to civilians. McCann's training, as well as his books and instructional videos, is simply outstanding. If you're serious about self-protection, you owe it to yourself to look into it.

FASTDefense.com – Bill Kipp is one of the pioneers of adrenal stress training as it relates to civilian self-defense. His incredible courses allow you to experience the emotional and psychological elements of a real street attack, as well as the physiological effects they have on your ability to fight. In the process, you learn both verbal de-escalation and boundary setting and how to instantly escalate to physical combative skills when necessary. Kipp's hands-on courses are life-changing experiences and all of his training and support materials are among the best available.

Shivworks.com – This web site is home to the training schedule of Craig Douglas, aka "Southnarc."

A retired law enforcement officer with extensive undercover narcotics experience, Douglas is also a highly accomplished martial artist. His courses focus on the violent realities of extreme-close-quarters attacks and the practical tactics necessary to survive them with empty hands, a knife, or a gun. His acclaimed "Managing Unknown Contacts" course teaches how to recognize and manage the pre-incident indicators that precede most street attacks and is *the* standard of excellence on this topic. All of Douglas' training is based on his hard-won knowledge and comes highly recommended.

ABOUT THE AUTHOR

Michael Janich has been studying and teaching self-defense and the martial arts for more than 35 years. He has earned instructor's credentials in American Self-Protection (ASP – an eclectic art that includes elements of judo, aikido, boxing, fencing and French Savate), the Filipino art of Serrada Eskrima, and Joseph Simonet's Silat Concepts and is a member of the elite International Close-Combat Instructors' Association. He has also trained extensively in wing chun gung fu, tae kwon do, wu ying tao, Thai boxing, arnis de mano and military combatives. Janich is also one of the foremost modern authorities on handgun point shooting and is one of the few contemporary instructors to have been personally trained by the late close-combat legend Colonel Rex Applegate.

Janich served nine years in the U.S. Army Intelligence and Security Command, including a tour of duty at the National Security Agency. He is a two-time graduate with honors of the Defense Language Institute in Monterey, California (Vietnamese and Chinese-Mandarin) and a recipient of the Commandant's Award for outstanding linguistic achievement. After completing his military service, Janich was recruited by the Defense Intelligence Agency (DIA) and served as an Intelligence Officer for that agency's Stony Beach Program in Hong Kong and the Philippines. He also served as an Investigation Team Leader for the Joint Casualty Resolution Center (JCRC) and Joint Task Force-Full Accounting (JTF-FA) and has led numerous investigations into remote areas of Vietnam and Laos in search of information regarding American prisoners of war and missing in action (POW/MIA).

In 1994, Janich founded Paladin Press' video production department. During the 10 years that followed, he shot, directed, and edited more than 100 instructional videos on all aspects of self-defense, close-combat, and related topics. He personally recruited and worked with some of the leading instructors in the tactical industry, including Kelly McCann, James Keating, the late Jim Cirillo, Louis Awerbuck, John Plaster, and the late Col. Rex Applegate.

Janich is the sole author of six books and co-author of seven, including Bullseyes Don't Shoot Back, which he wrote with the late close-combat legend Col. Rex Applegate. He has also been featured in more than 20 instructional videos on defensive edged-weapon use, use of the Filipino balisong knife, the use of throwing weapons and exotic weapons, stick fighting, and combat shooting. In addition to books and videos, Janich has been published in more than a dozen magazines and newsletters and is a columnist and contributing editor to *Tactical Knives* magazine. His television appearances include *Ripley's Believe It or Not*, multiple appearances on the Outdoor Channel's *Shooting Gallery*, and SPIKE TV's *Don't Be a Victim*, and a feature appearance on the Discovery Channel's *Time Warp*. He is also the co-host of the Outdoor Channel's *The Best Defense* and *The Best Defense: Survival!*

Janich is the author and co-author of numerous books, including *Bullseyes Don't Shoot Back*, which he wrote with the late close-combat legend Col. Rex Applegate. A prolific knife designer, Janich has also designed both custom and production knives for the Masters of Defense knife company, BlackHawk Blades, Spyderco, Combat Elite, and several noted custom makers. In addition to his teaching and writing activities, he currently serves as the Special Projects Coordinator for the Spyderco knife company of Golden, Colorado.

Made in the USA
Las Vegas, NV
12 January 2024